Michelle & Jim.
   Thanks for all our
doggy sitting.
      Love
         Joan & John
           X X X
            X X
             X

GOOD DOG!

GOOD DOG!

The Basic Training Book for All Breeds

JACK HOWELL, MBE

FARMING PRESS LIMITED
WHARFEDALE ROAD IPSWICH SUFFOLK

FIRST EDITION 1977

SECOND IMPRESSION 1977

ISBN 0 85236 078 9

*This book is set in 10pt on 12pt type and is printed in Great Britain
on Nimrod coated cartridge paper by The Lavenham Press Limited,
Lavenham, Suffolk.*

TO ARTHUR M. REES FOR HIS KINDNESS,
ENCOURAGEMENT AND ASSISTANCE OVER
MANY YEARS

Contents

4. CRIMINAL WORK

The Chase and Attack — The Stand-off Exercise — The Attack under Gunfire — Attack on Criminal Armed with a Stick or Other Weapon

5. TRAINING FOR DEMONSTRATION PURPOSES

The Fire Hoop — The Fire Bell — Carrying the Fire Bucket — Selecting Named Flags — The Cycle Act — The Dog in the Pram — 'The End' Board

APPENDIX

INDEX

Illustrations

Photograph on page 15 shows the author with two of his dogs and some of the many cups and trophies won in competitions.

Foreword

By Mr Arthur Rees, CBE, QPM, MA, DL,
Chief Constable of Staffordshire

EX CHIEF INSPECTOR Jack Howell was the founder of the Police Dog Training School at Police Headquarters, Stafford, where he remained as the chief instructor and officer-in-charge for some twenty years until his retirement from the force. During that time about two thousand handlers and dogs have passed through the school, not only from police forces in Great Britain but from practically every corner of the world, including Bahamas, Bermuda, Barbados, St. Lucia, Montserrat, Trinidad and Tobago, Nigeria, Uganda, Cameroons, Jordan, Malta, Lebanon, Luxembourg, Tanzania, Pakistan, Lesotho, Sweden, Seychelles, Hong Kong and Australia.

Mr Howell has trained many national champions from the police and prison service dogs, including the first-ever Champion Police Dog of Great Britain. He is a national judge and long-standing member of the Home Office Advisory Committee on Police Dog Training, and has travelled extensively to other countries where he has acted as adviser on the use and training of police dogs. His very wide knowledge and lifetime experience of dogs and their training will, I am sure, be of great help to those who read this book which he has written in easy-to-follow terms covering all aspects of dog training.

Stafford
January, 1977

A. M. REES

Introduction

IN THE following pages I hope to help not only the owners who wish to train their dogs in general obedience, but also those who intend to reach the higher standards of tracking, searching for property, searching for hidden persons, agility and criminal work. In the final chapter I shall explain how the training for some of the more spectacular exercises in dog demonstrations for the general public is done.

Any breed of dog can be successfully trained. It need not be a pedigree one, for an ordinary mongrel can be trained equally as well as a highly pedigreed dog.

Some dogs are naturally more responsive to training than others, but it does not necessarily follow that a dog which accepts the training and responds quickly is more intelligent than others. Quite often it is the reverse, and it is the more intelligent animal which is dubious of a new training exercise.

There are some dogs which cannot be trained to a very high standard, such as the extremely nervous ones and of course dogs which are in one way or another physically unsuitable. For example, a very small dog could be well trained in obedience, but there would be some difficulty in some of the criminal work exercises.

Some dogs are nervous simply because they have not been brought up in the correct environment; as a result they have not been allowed to come in contact with people, traffic and indeed the hustle and bustle of modern-day life. This type of nervousness can usually be corrected by careful and sensible handling. Other dogs have an inbred nervousness which usually remains throughout their lives. Regrettably, there are also dogs which are nervous because of ill-treatment, but this too can be corrected by kind and sensible handling, although in some cases it may take some considerable time.

Temperament is most important, and in this respect the most suitable type of animal is the one which is bold and fearless but at the same time good-tempered.

The most suitable age for the dog to commence a training course is between eight months and two years, for by this time it is old enough to understand and strong enough to undergo the training. There is no hard and fast rule, however,

13

for some dogs mature much more quickly than others and it may therefore be possible to start the training a little earlier than eight months.

Although eight months to two years is the most suitable age group, much older dogs can be successfully trained and the old saying that you cannot teach an old dog new tricks is not entirely true. However, a dog which is over two years of age may cause a few more problems than one which is rather younger.

A young puppy which is too young to commence a training course should be allowed to see as much as possible, to mix freely with people and animals and to become accustomed to traffic and noise.

From an early age the puppy should be taught to refrain from doing something contrary to your wishes when the command 'NO' is given. The command should be given in a firm and commanding voice and any physical correction should be given at the same time as the command. The command is a very important one which it will be necessary to use from time to time throughout the dog's training and indeed throughout its life.

A young puppy between the age of eight weeks and eight months should be encouraged to pick up and carry articles of various kinds as this will be a great help when the retrieve and other exercises are commenced later on. It is a simple matter to teach a puppy to pick up and carry articles but much more difficult when it is older and has not been encouraged to do so in its early days.

Although a young dog or puppy may be below the required training age, it should be given a certain amount of discipline but nevertheless allowed to develop its own character. Like humans, dogs have their own individual characters. There are the extroverts and introverts, the happy-go-lucky ones and the steady, easy-going ones. There are no two which are exactly alike, and the character of the dog must be taken into consideration during the training. Some dogs, for example, need a lot of praise, whilst others are quite satisfied with the odd pat on the head when they have done something to please you. Some dogs are very easily snubbed, whilst others are exactly the opposite.

Basic Principles

There are certain basic principles which must be known and adhered to at all times, for without them it will not be possible to train your dog. For example, it would be wrong to commence to train a dog which does not know you. If you try to discipline a strange dog, it will not only resent you but it will also resent the training. It is therefore important that the dog should know you and that there is a strong bond of affection between yourself and the dog before training can begin.

Many people carry out long one-way conversations with their dogs, and it is common to hear people say that their dogs understand every word they say. Dogs connect certain words with certain actions but they can not understand English or any other language so do not expect them to do so! Use the correct word of command for the exercise in hand and do not waste your time addressing your dog at length, which only confuses it. For example, if you give

14

The author with two of his dogs and some of the many cups and trophies won in competitions.

the command 'STAND' every time you make the dog sit, it will only sit on the command 'STAND'.

It is quite surprising how many people punish their dog for what they think is disobedience when in fact it has misunderstood the command. It is far better to let the dog get away with something than punish misunderstanding.

Misunderstanding should never be the cause of punishment, but deliberate disobedience should be corrected at once. It is usually sufficient to punish the dog by tone of voice or at the most by taking hold of its neck on either side and giving it a good shake. Severe punishment should only be used in very exceptional circumstances.

When a dog has done well it should simply be rewarded by praise. A dog loves to please its owner and will work all the better if it is praised. But only praise it when it has done something well.

Dogs quickly become bored, so do not prolong an exercise that could cause tiredness or boredom. Change to another exercise or give it a rest. It is also wrong to nag continually at a dog, for it cannot concentrate on the exercise if it is being flustered.

By all means take advice from experienced handlers and trainers, but remember that there are probably more self-appointed experts in the dog world than any other field, and wrong advice can quickly ruin all that you have done.

Always be patient, kind but at all times firm, and whatever you do you must never let the dog get away with deliberate disobedience. If you do, it will try again and again and you will be wasting your time.

15

A dog will not train itself, and you must be prepared to work hard and give it the desired attention and training. The training must be consistent and regular and you must try to spend as much time as possible each day.

The dog must have plenty of exercise each day in addition to its training. Always finish a particular exercise when it has done it well, but if it is having difficulty, it is advisable to change to another exercise which you know it can accomplish and then finish.

A DOG IS AS GOOD AS ITS OWNER. MAKE SURE THAT YOU HAVE A GOOD DOG.

The photographs in this book are mostly of Alsatians at a Police Dog Training Centre, but the methods advocated apply to all breeds and indeed mongrels.

1

General Obedience

Heel Work on the Lead

THE FIRST exercise to teach the dog will be heel work on the lead. The dog is taught to walk close to your left side without lagging behind, pulling to one side or going too far forward.

The dog's right shoulder should be as close to your left knee as possible, and when performing this exercise the dog should always be in a happy frame of mind. On no account should it slink along as though it has no interest in you or the exercise.

A fairly long lead and a check chain should be used for this exercise, but great care should be taken when using the check chain, and continuous pulling and snatching at the dog's neck should be avoided at all costs.

It is very important to place the check chain on the dog in the correct manner so that it will slacken off when there is no pressure on the lead (*photos 1 and 2*).

Commence the exercise with the dog at your left side and hold the lead in your right hand, which should be about waist high in the centre of the body. The lead should form a slight loop and should not be held tight.

Move forward with the dog, giving a slight jerk on the lead, at the same time

1. *Check chain correct.*

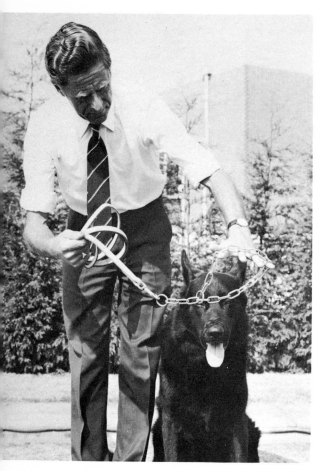

2. *Check chain incorrect.*

from you at the slightest movement of your hand.

Make a series of left, right and about turns giving the command 'HEEL' on each turn. You will never be able to teach the dog to do heel work by walking in a straight line all the time.

When the dog is close to your left side, the lead must be slack so that there is no discomfort to the dog. If, however, the dog tends to pull away from you it will be necessary to give the lead a sharp jerk, at the same time giving the command 'HEEL'.

Do not try to pull or drag the dog along on the lead as it will cause the animal to pull against you. A sharp jerk or snatch is

3. *Heel work on the lead.*

giving the command 'HEEL'. Walk fairly quickly, taking short bouncy steps rather than long strides (*photo 3*).

Your left hand is kept free of the lead and you should use this hand to encourage the dog to keep close. This can be done by tapping your left side or some similar movement. Quite often it will help if you carry a small article in your left hand, such as a small stick or a piece of cloth in which the dog is interested.

Do not grab at the dog with your left, or indeed your right hand, as this will tend to make it hand-shy and it will pull away all that is needed, with the lead being slackened off immediately the dog is close and in the correct position.

As the training improves, the jerks or snatches should become lighter and of course less frequent until finally this correction is no longer needed. When this stage is reached, the lead should be held as previously described but so lightly that the dog will feel no pressure whatsoever.

A dog which tends to lag behind on heel work should be encouraged as much as possible by both voice and hand. The lead must be slack and you must alter your pace frequently from normal to fast and slow. It is emphasised that much encouragement is needed and snatching and pulling on the lead avoided. Give the dog lots of praise when it is keeping close so that it quickly realises that it is pleasing you.

If the dog pulls ahead of you, it must be corrected by jerking the lead upwards and backwards and giving the command 'HEEL'. When the dog is in the correct position, the lead must be slackened at once. On no account should the lead be pulled or snatched across the front of your body to correct a dog which is pulling ahead.

If the dog persistently pulls ahead of you it can be corrected by doing frequent about turns, which will leave it either in the correct heel position or slightly behind you.

Quite often the dog will be inclined to walk at an angle, with its hind-quarters slightly away from your side. This fault can be corrected by walking in a sort of zig-zag manner, giving the dog as much encouragement as possible.

As the heel work training progresses, it is possible to encourage the dog to keep closer to your left side if you step off with the left foot and place the left foot over the right one (*photo 4*). In other words, you

4. *Stepping off at an angle in the heel work exercise.*

step off at an angle. By doing a series of these inclines to your right, at the same time giving the command 'HEEL', the dog will pay more attention to you and as a result it will be inclined to keep closer to your left side.

It is very important that you vary the pace during heel work training from ordinary walking pace to fast and slow. By doing this you will cause the dog to concentrate and become more alert.

Remember that the dog must keep as close to your left leg as possible, regardless of the left, right and about turns. It must keep equally as close on the turns as it does when walking in a straight line.

19

On the about turn you should make the turn slowly in order to give the dog time to go round you and to enable it to keep close. As soon as the turn has been made, you should quicken your pace, taking several short quick steps and encouraging the dog as you do so. Later on, when the dog is proficient at heel work, it will be possible to make the about turns much more quickly. A quick jerk on the lead is needed as the turn is made and of course the command 'HEEL' should be given.

The right turn should be done in very much the same manner as the about turn. Make the turn slowly and deliberately, giving the slight jerk on the lead as the turn is made and at the same time the command 'HEEL'.

The left turn can sometimes cause a few problems in the early stages of the training and it sometimes happens that owners actually fall over their dogs in the process. To encourage and obtain a good left turn, you should slow down but lengthen your pace just before making the turn; this will put the dog in the correct position for a neat and tidy turn. If the dog is in a forward position when the turn is made, it can be corrected by bending the right knee and bringing it round quickly in order to catch the dog on the nose, thus bringing it back into the correct heel position.

Another method of training for the left turn is to do a series of tight circles to your left, placing the right foot in front of the left one as you make the turns and encouraging the dog as much as possible to keep close.

During the heel work sessions you should continue the exercise as long as the dog is showing interest and no longer. Dogs quickly become bored and if this is the case you should give the dog a rest.

As the heel work training progresses, the sit, down and stand exercises may be introduced when you come to a halt and

5. *Teaching the dog to sit at heel.*

you will commence with the sit exercise.

As you come to a halt you should jerk the lead upwards above the dog's head and with the left hand push the dog into the sit position by pressure on the hind-quarters, giving the command 'SIT' in a firm and positive manner as you do so.

As in all commands, a command should only be given once if the dog responds and not repeated three or four times as many owners often do. If repeated commands are given, the dog will expect it and it will only complete the exercise if it has been told a number of times.

It is important that the dog should be sitting correctly in line with you and of course facing in the same direction.

Quite often the dog will not be sitting correctly; it will either be too far away, or the fore-quarters will be correct and the hind-quarters at an angle away from you.

The dog must not be allowed to get away

20

with incorrect 'sits' or indeed with any other incorrect position, and faults of this nature must be corrected immediately.

To correct a bad sitting position, you should bend your knees, place your left hand over the dog and guide it into the correct position (*photo 5*).

Heel work should be practised daily, and you should spend as much time as possible with the dog, making sure of course that it does not become tired or bored. There will be a marked improvement if only about fifteen minutes are spent on the exercise each day, but try to spend much longer if you possibly can. Be extremely patient, and although you must be kind, you must also be firm. Always aim for perfection and remember that nothing less will do.

Heel-free Exercise

When the dog has become proficient at heel work on the lead, it should be walking to heel in a correct and happy manner with the lead held loosely so that there is no pressure whatsoever on the dog's neck. It will now be time to commence the heel-work-off-the-lead exercise.

Commence with the dog in the sit position, and as your move forward, give the command 'HEEL'. Encourage the dog as you go along, just as you did in the previous exercise. Continue to make the dog sit when you come to a halt (*photo 6*).

In all probability, when the dog is taken off the lead for this exercise, it will try to take advantage and go away from you. Do not make a grab at it or run after it but simply encourage it to come to you and continue the heel work exercise, attracting its attention as you did during the training on the lead. In any case you will never get the dog to come to you by running after it, you will be more successful by running away from it and at the same time calling it.

Providing that the dog has mastered the heel work on the lead exercise properly, there should not be any great difficulty with the heel work off the lead. Continue to work the dog on the lead from time to time and try to make as little fuss as possible when you take the lead off.

As before, you must make frequent turns, encourage the dog as much as possible and try to attract its attention. The stage will eventually be reached when the dog will walk freely and happily at your side without any commands, attractions or encouragement.

The Down Exercise

As with the sit and stand, the down exercise is commenced with the dog in the

6. *Sitting at heel.*

21

heel position, on the lead and at your left side. You have already taught the dog to sit at heel, so place it in the sit position. Place your left hand on the dog's back just behind the shoulders, and with a backward movement of the hand gently press downwards, at the same time pulling the dog into the down position by using a shortened lead in the right hand (*photo 7*). The command 'DOWN' should be given simultaneously with the pressure from the lead and left hand.

Do not use more than one command such as lie down, sit down and so on, only the command 'DOWN'. The command should be given in a firm clear voice as though you are telling it to go down, not asking it.

Another method of teaching the dog the down exercise is to kneel in front of it, take the lead in the right hand close to the check chain and pull the dog into the down position, at the same time placing the left arm under the forelegs and gently easing

7. *Teaching the dog the down exercise.*

them forward. Do not forget to give the command 'DOWN' at the same time.

Spend as much time as possible on the down exercise until the dog is responding to the word of command, but do not neglect the heel work on and off the lead and the sit exercise.

The Stand Exercise

Commence this exercise with the dog sitting at heel and on the lead. Place the left arm over the dog's back and with the hand under the centre of its body, gently raise the dog into the stand position, at the same time giving the command 'STAND' (*photo 8*). This method can be incorporated into the heel work exercise, as also can the sit and the down, so that when you come to

8. *Teaching the dog to stand at heel.*

22

a halt on the heel work you can alternate between the three exercises of sit, down and stand.

Do not continue to lift the dog into the stand position once it is responding to the command and always make sure that it is standing close to your left side and facing the correct way. Do not let the dog get away with crooked sits, downs and stands.

Distance Control

Having mastered the heel-on-lead, heel free, and sit, down and stand-at-heel exercises, it is now time to commence the distance control and this will include the stay in addition to the sit, down and stand positions. This means that you will be able to put your dog in any of the three positions and also that it will stay in any given position at a distance from you.

Later on, it will be necessary to teach the dog to come to you when called, but although this is a very important exercise it must not be attempted until the stay has

been mastered. I have mentioned this at this stage because so many trainers and owners are inclined to teach the recall much too soon, and as a result, other exercises are either ruined or at the least made much more difficult.

The Stay Exercise

The object of this exercise is to teach the dog to stay in either the down, sit or stand positions, even when you are out of sight of the dog. It is not a very difficult exercise providing that the dog has reached a good standard in all the exercises so far. As with all other exercises, however, much patience will be needed, and you must be prepared to spend as much time as possible without causing the dog to become bored.

The word of command is 'STAY', and although it has not been necessary to use hand signals for any of the exercises so far, they should be used for the stay and other exercises involving distance control.

For the stay exercise, the hand signal is

9. *Hand signals when teaching the dog to stay.*

similar to the one used to stop an on-coming vehicle. In other words, the right arm is held in front of the body, about chest high, with the hand open and the palm facing the dog (*photo 9*).

Commence the exercise with the dog at heel, on the lead and in the down position. Holding the lead in the left hand, turn and face the dog and slowly back away. Give the hand signal as previously described and the word of command, 'STAY'. If the dog remains in the down position when the lead is fully extended, do not repeat the command but simply stand in front of it for a couple of minutes and then return to it by walking round its left side and back to the correct heel position (*photo 10*). Gently praise the dog but do not overdo it as excessive praise will cause the dog to get excited and it will get up and move.

If the dog begins to get up when you are standing in front of it, it must be corrected by making it adopt the down position by use of the lead, at the same time giving the appropriate command and signal.

As the training in this exercise improves, the lead should be gently placed on the ground in front of the dog and you should back away for a further yard or so. If the dog again stays in the down position without moving, return to it after a few minutes as before but do not on any account call the dog to you at this stage. Gradually increase the distance between yourself and the dog but do not get too far away at first. The training should be gradual and on no account should it be rushed.

In addition to increasing the distance between yourself and the dog, you should also slowly increase the time that you are away from it.

As progress is made, it will no longer be necessary to have the lead attached to the dog and instead of backing away from it, you should be able to walk away in the normal manner. Keep your eye on the dog

10. *Walking round the dog and back to the correct heel position.*

at all times so that you can correct it quickly if it gets up or attempts to move.

The stay-in-the-sit and stay-in-the-stand positions should not cause any great problems once you have mastered the stay-in-the-down position. The dog will not be quite so comfortable in these positions, however, and it cannot be expected to remain in them for long periods.

Commence the stay-sit and stay-stand

24

exercises in the same manner as the stay-down, with the lead attached. Do not on any account try to rush the training and do not be tempted to go too far away from the dog in the initial stages.

Finally, when the dog is really doing well in the stay exercise, you should walk away and adopt a position where you can see the dog but it is unable to see you. If you do this, you will be able to correct it at once if it moves.

Do not continually use the same training area for this exercise, or the dog will become accustomed to staying only when it is in that particular area. When the dog is doing well, it should be left in areas which are unfamiliar to it and distractions should be introduced, such as people and animals walking about in close proximity. Always go back to the dog, as described earlier. Do not allow it to get up or move into another position as you return to it. It should always remain in the position you left it in until you give a further command.

To finish the exercise you should stand by the dog in the correct heel position, pause for a little while and then take one step forward, bringing the dog into the

11. *Teaching the sit from a distance.*

12. *Teaching the down from a distance.*

sit-at-heel position. Always praise the dog when it has done well.

Continue to practice all the exercises you have done so far.

Distance Control:
Sit, Down and Stand

Distance control simply means that you are able to control your dog from a distance, placing it in either the sit, down or stand positions. A well-trained dog should respond at a distance of at least one hundred metres but this will only be achieved by patience, perseverance, hard work and common sense.

You have already taught the dog the sit, down and stand exercises at heel, and also the stay in all three positions, and as a result you should not have any great difficulty in teaching it the distance control.

Commence with the dog in the down position. Stand in front of the dog, holding the full length of the lead in the left hand. Give the command 'SIT', at the same time giving a hand signal with the right hand. This is done by raising the right arm sharply and pointing in an upward direction (*photo 11*). If the dog does not respond at once, repeat the command and signal and at the same time jerk the lead upwards to lift the dog into the sit position. Quickly correct the dog if it moves, giving the command and signal.

When the dog has been sitting for about two minutes, you should return it to the down position. The word of command is 'DOWN' and the hand signal is more or less the opposite to the one used for the sit. Using the right arm, point in a downwards direction, bending the body slightly as you do so (*photo 12*). If the dog does not respond, you should repeat the command and signal and at the same time jerk the lead downwards to cause the dog to adopt the down position. Leave the dog in the down position for a few minutes, and then

26

13. *Teaching the dog to stand from a distance.*

return it to the sit position in the manner previously described.

When alternating between the sit and down you should vary the pause between the two exercises and on no account should you cause the dog to change its position without a pause.

The stand exercise will be a little more difficult than the sit and down, but as you have already taught the dog to stand at heel and also mastered the stay exercise it should not create any great problems.

With the dog in the sit position, stand in front of it as before, holding the lead in the left hand. There are a number of hand signals which can be used but a suitable one is to bring the right arm outwards and then inwards, with the palm of the hand finally resting on the chest (*photo 13*). The word of command is 'STAND'.

There should not be any forward movement from the dog when it comes into the stand position and it is therefore important that the initial training is done in a correct manner.

Giving the command 'STAND' and the appropriate hand signal, gently pull the dog into the stand position by use of the lead. As already mentioned, the lead should be in the left hand and the signal given by the right hand. You must be extremely careful not to pull the dog forward during the training, for if you do, it will obviously think that it is doing the correct thing by moving forward and it will be difficult to eradicate the fault.

Leave the dog in the stand position for about thirty seconds and then return it to the sit or down position. Pause for a little while before repeating the stand exercise.

27

When the dog is responding to your command and signal without pressure from the lead, you should gently place the lead on the ground and back away for a few paces. If the dog does not respond now that you are further away and are no longer holding the lead, it will be necessary to move forward and place it in the desired position by use of the lead, as previously described. If, however, the dog reacts favourably, then you can continue the training and gradually move further and further away. Finally, the lead can be removed and you can walk away in the normal manner, about turn, face the dog and after a pause place the dog in either the sit or down position.

I must again stress the point that you must not command the dog to change its position immediately you turn to face it. If you do this, it will begin to anticipate and it will change its position as soon as you turn to face it, without being told to do so.

I have already said that there should not be any forward movement from the dog when it is being placed in the stand position, and naturally this applies to the sit and down exercises too. It sometimes helps if the dog is placed on a stout table or similar article when the distance control exercises are being carried out so that it is unable to move forward without jumping off.

Another method is to place an object of some kind in front of the dog to form a barrier. The object should be large enough to check the forward movement but, naturally, not too large to obstruct either your vision or that of the dog (*photo 14*).

During the distance control exercises

14. *Distance control being carried out with the dog behind a barrier. The stay signal is being used.*

28

you should return to the dog and adopt the heel-free position when the training ends.

The Recall Exercise

Provided that the dog has reached a good standard in the previous training exercises, particularly the stay and distance control, the recall exercise can commence.

The ultimate aim is to get the dog to return to you from a distance when called. It should return immediately and happily, at a good speed, and sit closely in front (*photo 15*). After a pause and on the command 'HEEL' it should go round you and finish in the sit-at-heel position.

It is emphasised that at no time should the dog associate coming to you with something unpleasant. It must always be fun and enjoyment to the dog and at the same time it must be aware that you too are pleased. It is therefore extremely important that the dog is never scolded when it has come to you, even though it may have taken some time to get it to do so. It cannot be expected to understand that it has been rebuked for taking its time and naturally it connects the scolding with returning to you. It follows, therefore, that it will be reluctant to come to you the next time it is called.

Dogs which are kept in kennels can quickly associate the recall with something which is unpleasant if they are allowed their freedom, recalled and immediately returned to their kennels. Naturally they prefer a good romp around and their freedom to being placed in kennels, no matter how good their quarters may be.

It is of course very important that the dog is allowed its freedom, but to avoid difficulties with the recall exercise it is better to call the dog, give it some other training which it enjoys and then return it to its sleeping quarters.

The word of command for the recall

15. *Sitting in front after recall.*

exercise is 'COME' and this may be preceded by the dog's name. A suitable hand signal which should not clash with any future ones is to raise both arms to shoulder height and then return them to the side in one complete movement (*photo 16*).

Commence the exercise with the dog in

29

16. *Hand signals for the recall exercise.*

either the sit or down position and walk
away for a distance of about twenty paces.
Turn and face the dog and after a pause,
give the command and hand signal, at the
same time calling the dog's name. The
command should be given in an encouraging tone of voice rather than a strict command. It is not advisable to call the dog
from the stand position in the early stages
of the recall training, as this would encourage it to come forward when being
placed in the stand position at a distance
from you. It would also have an adverse
effect on the stay-stand exercise.

If the dog comes to you when called, do
not attempt to make it sit in front of you
for the first few times, as the prime consideration at this stage is to get it to return.
Once the dog is responding to your command and signal the finishing touches can
be put to the exercise. In other words, it
can be placed in the sit position in front of
you and after a pause, and on the command
'HEEL', guided round you to the sit-at-
heel position. Remember to give the dog

lots of praise when it comes to you.

Some dogs are reluctant to return at
first and this is to be expected, for the
simple reason that you have been con-
centrating on the stay and distance control
exercises up to now and the dog is a little
confused. However, with much encouragement and by adopting a crouching position,
it will be possible to get the dog to come to
you.

It is possible that the dog will come
towards you and then stop before it reaches
you. If this is the case with your dog, you
should take a few steps backwards as you
continue to encourage it and then halt
abruptly in front of it when it is close.

Other dogs are so boisterous and full of
enthusiasm when called that they are
inclined to run past you. This can be
corrected by advancing towards the dog as
it approaches and again halting suddenly
in front of it.

Another method of teaching the recall is
to leave the dog in the sit or down position
with a long line attached to its check

chain. After turning to face the dog, pause for a short time and as you give the command and hand signal, give the line a gentle pull (*photo 17*). Gently guide the dog to you but be very careful not to snatch at the line. Praise the dog when it gets to you.

Do not on any account overdo the recall training or you may ruin all that you have done in the stay and distance control exercises. In other words, do not do the recall time after time but simply do one or two recalls and then change to another exercise.

During the training for the recall exercise you should adopt a comfortable position with the legs slightly apart in order that the dog can move in closely and not develop the bad habit of sitting too far away.

When the dog is returning to you freely and happily on command, it will be time to teach it to sit properly in front and after a

pause, to go round you to the sit-at-heel position on your left side. To get the dog to sit it will be necessary to give the command 'SIT' at first, but after a little while it should begin to sit automatically.

The next stage is to teach the dog to change its position from the sit-in-front to the sit-at-heel position. The word of command is 'HEEL'. Give the command, and holding the end of the check chain in the right hand, guide the dog round you from your right to left side. As the dog comes round the back of you, it will be necessary to change the chain over to the left hand in order to keep the dog close and to bring it to the correct sit-at-heel position.

The coming-to-heel exercise from the sit-in-front, can be practised as a separate exercise if need be, without it being incorporated into the recall exercise. In this case the dog is placed in the sit-in-front position with the lead attached and is

17. *Teaching the recall with line attached.*

18. *Bringing the dog to heel from the sit-in-front position.*

need to practice it as a separate exercise and it can be incorporated into the full recall exercise.

It is emphasised that much patience will be needed during the training for the recall exercise and on no account should the dog be punished or scolded after it has been recalled.

Continue to give the dog its training in all the exercises so far and do not neglect any of them.

The Retrieve Exercise

The dog has an inherent instinct to retrieve, dating back to its wild state when it had to carry the carcases of other animals back to its lair in order to survive. This natural instinct has been developed in the domesticated dog so that it will pick up and carry articles of various kinds.

Because of this natural instinct most dogs are interested in retrieving, particularly so if the dog has been encouraged to pick up and carry articles from an early age as suggested in the early pages of this book.

There are of course some dogs which have been scolded in their early days for doing so. Naturally, it will be a little more difficult to teach these dogs to retrieve, but with much encouragement and correct training the problem will be in no way unsurmountable.

The ultimate aim in this exercise is to have the dog off the lead and sitting at heel on your left side. An article is either thrown or placed in front of the dog and on the command 'FETCH', and not before, the dog should run out, pick up the article cleanly and without undue mouthing or chewing, carry the article back to you and sit closely and squarely in front as it did in the recall exercise. After the dog has picked up the article, it must not drop it but should continue to hold it until you take the article from it on the command

directed to the sit-at-heel position by use of the lead instead of the check chain. Remember to keep the dog as close to you as possible as it moves round you from the sit-in-front to sit-at-heel position (*photo 18*), and also make sure that it sits close and squarely on completion of the exercise at your left side. When the dog is responding to your command, there will be no

'LEAVE'. The dog should give up the article immediately the command is given. After a pause, and on the command 'HEEL', the dog should return to its original position at heel, again as it did in the recall exercise.

Commence the exercise with the dog on a fairly long training lead, sitting at heel. Throw out an article, preferably a dumbbell, although a piece of wood or a small piece of rubber hose or something similar will no doubt be all right. Give the command 'FETCH' in an encouraging tone of voice, and holding the end of the lead, allow the dog to run out and pick up the article. When the dog has picked up the article, gently guide the animal to you and back away a few paces as you do so (*photo 19*). When the dog is close, halt abruptly in front of it and give the command

'SIT'. Allow the dog to hold the article for a little while, taking into consideration how well it is holding it. Give the command 'LEAVE' and take the article from the dog using both hands, one on either side of the object.

Care should be taken not to cause any pain or discomfort to the dog when you take the article. After a pause, which should be varied in length each time the exercise is done, the dog should be given the command 'HEEL' and placed in the sit at heel position. Give the dog lots of praise.

As the training improves, the next stage is to remove the lead. With the dog sitting at heel, throw out the article for a distance of about ten paces and give the command 'FETCH'. If the dog responds and returns with it to sit in front of you, remember to

19. *Teaching the retrieve.*

33

pause for a short time before taking the article, and after a further pause bring the dog to the sit-at-heel position. It is very important that you praise the dog.

It is possible of course that there will be a few problems, and that instead of returning with the article, the dog will decide to tear about with the article in its mouth. If this happens, you should encourage the dog to come to you and at the same time back away quickly. This will help to attract its attention to you, and with patience and perseverance you should be able to get it to return. When the dog is close to you, you should halt suddenly in front of it and give the command 'SIT'. Finish the exercise as before by bringing the dog to the sit-at-heel position and again praise the dog.

It is also possible that the dog will begin to come towards you with the article but stop before it reaches you and refuse to come further. If this is the case, you should again take a few backward steps to encourage it to come to you and then halt in front of the dog when it is close. As always give the dog plenty of praise when it has done well.

If, on its return, the dog drops the article at your feet, you should take up the article and gently place it in the animal's mouth, at the same time giving the command 'HOLD IT'. It will help if you place the palm of your hand under the mouth in order to lift the dog's head slightly, thus assisting it in holding the article. Each time the dog drops the article return it to its mouth, giving the command 'HOLD IT'. After a while the dog will realise that it must hold the article until the command 'LEAVE' is given (*photo 20*). Do not prolong the exercise until the dog becomes bored.

Many owners use the command 'HOLD' rather than 'HOLD IT', but because 'HOLD' is similar in sound to 'NO' it can

20. *Taking the article after the retrieve.*

cause considerable confusion to the dog, and the training will suffer as a result.

It sometimes helps if the training for the retrieve exercise is done in an entry, passageway or similar place, where the dog is restricted as to its movements and as a result it is much easier to get it to return.

Once the dog is doing well on the retrieve exercise, you should not continue to take any backward steps and it should not be necessary to give the command 'SIT' when it reaches you. If you continue

34

to step backwards, the dog will become to expect it and you will not achieve the desired results. Likewise, if you continue to tell the dog to sit, it will always expect it and will not sit on its own accord. For a perfect retrieve the only commands which should be given are 'FETCH', 'LEAVE' and 'HEEL'.

A dog which is not interested in picking up an article will obviously need much encouragement. If your dog is like this, you will require to persevere and have a considerable amount of patience. Select an article which is likely to interest the dog, such as a rolled-up piece of cloth, an old rabbit skin or something similar. With the dog on the lead, throw the article for a short distance and run with the dog towards it, giving the command 'FETCH' in an encouraging tone of voice. Kick the article about for the dog to chase after it in play. If it shows the slightest interest, give it plenty of praise. Once you have been able to get it to pick up and carry the article you can commence the training as described earlier.

With a difficult recall dog, the initial training for the retrieve can be done with the dog on a long line. Make sure that you do not snatch at the line, however, as this will cause the dog to drop the article. The dog must be gently guided to you and not forced.

If you are having considerable difficulty in getting the dog to return to you, then it may be necessary for you to leave the retrieve for a little longer in order that the recall exercise is improved.

During the retrieve exercise training, great care should be taken to avoid any misunderstanding by the dog. For example, if you punish it for dropping the article, it is likely to connect the punishment with the retrieve exercise generally and not with the dropping of the article. The punishment would therefore have an adverse effect on the whole of the retrieve training.

Do not exercise your dog by throwing an article and allowing it to chase about with it. You can not expect the dog to read your mind and to know when it can run about in such a manner and when it should do a correct retrieve. If you wish to give it the exercise by retrieving, by all means do so but make sure that the retrieve is done in the proper way.

Some trainers use the compulsory method to teach to dog to retrieve. In other words, the dog is compelled to hold the article by pressure on its mouth. This type of training can produce an unhappy retrieving dog and as a result it will reflect on its work, particularly the search for articles exercise which will be explained later.

The Speak-on-Command Exercise

This exercise simply means that the dog should bark when commanded to do so. The word of command is 'SPEAK'.

There are a number of ways to teach this exercise and if you will have patience and persevere, good results can be achieved in a very short time.

One method is to place the dog in the sit position. Kneel in front of it and with the palm of the hand commence to tap it under the lower jaw, at the same time giving the command 'SPEAK'. Continue to do this until eventually the dog becomes frustrated, when it will probably give a little squeak at first rather than a bark. If it does this, however, you should praise it profusely and give it a rest before repeating the exercise. With continued training on these lines it should be possible to get the dog to bark properly by command only.

A dog can be taught to bark by giving the command 'SPEAK' and withholding its food. As in the previous method, the dog becomes frustrated and will eventually

21. *Pushing the dog over on its side.*

command 'CEASE'. If the command is given in a very firm and authoritative manner, it is usually sufficient to cause the dog to stop. If, however, the dog continues to bark, the command should be repeated and the hand placed round its mouth to check the barking.

The ultimate aim is to get the dog to speak on command whilst it is sitting in front of you, sitting at heel and walking at heel. It should not deviate from the position you have placed it in, and it must refrain from barking immediately the command 'CEASE' is given.

Teaching the Dog to Lie on its Side

A very interesting little exercise, which is quite easy to teach, effective and indeed most useful, is what I call the lie exercise.

The dog is taught to lie on its side at a distance from you on the command 'LIE'. A suitable hand signal is to hold the right hand in front of you with the hand open and the palm downwards. Move the hand in a short sweeping movement either to the left or right according to which way you require the dog to go over on its side.

To commence the training, leave the dog in the down position and stand immediately in front and facing it. Give the command 'LIE' and at the same time bend down and push the dog over on to its side (*photo* 21). You will have to be guided by the dog's position when deciding which way you want it to go over. Quite often a dog which is in the down position, will have its hind legs protruding to one side and it would therefore be quite simple to push it over on the opposite side.

As you push the dog over, the movement of your hand will be similar to the hand signal which you will eventually use when the dog is doing the exercise from a distance.

bark, although the bark may be a rather weak one at first. When the dog barks, give it its food and again lots of praise. This training can only be done at feeding times, however, and it is only successful with a dog which has a fairly good appetite.

A dog which is keen to retrieve can be taught the speak-on-command exercise by showing it a retrieve article of some kind. Instead of throwing or placing out the article, it should be held in front of you and out of reach of the dog. The command 'SPEAK' is given, and immediately the dog barks it should be praised and allowed to retrieve the article. After a while it should be possible to get the dog to speak on command without the aid of the article.

It will be noted that in all three methods the dog is induced to speak through frustration.

When the dog is responding to the 'SPEAK' on command, it will be necessary to stop it from barking by giving the

After you have pushed the dog over on its side, you should gently hold it in that position for a little while and then place it in the sit position. After a pause, return it to the down position and repeat the lie exercise.

Much firmness will be needed, and although you should praise the dog as you have done in all other training exercises, the praise should not be overdone, otherwise the dog will become excited and it will not remain calm in the lie position.

When the dog is responding on its own accord without being pushed into position, you should stand about one pace away and repeat the exercise, gradually going further away as training progresses (*photo 22*). Later on you should introduce distractions by walking back to the dog and stepping over it, correcting it at once if it should deviate from its position.

Although this exercise is not used in dog trials and competitions, it is a very useful one and when done properly it shows complete obedience and control. I consider that the exercise could well be introduced into obedience competitions and that it would be a step forward from the routine sits, downs and stands.

Agility

The dog is not a natural jumper; it either has to be taught, or through necessity it teaches itself.

The object of the following exercises is to teach the dog to jump and clear a hurdle, to clear a long jump and to scale a high board.

The height of the obstacles will always depend on the physical capabilities of the dog and this must be borne in mind during the training sessions. Some breeds are extremely agile and well suited to this type of training, whilst others are inclined to be rather cumbersome and awkward.

The training should be stopped immediately the dog shows signs of tiredness, and it should never be forced over obstacles that it is not physically capable of clearing.

The training should be done gradually and the height slowly increased, so that the

22. *Dog placed in the lie position at a distance from the handler.*

23. *Jumping the hurdle on the lead.*

dog builds up its confidence and physical condition at the same time.

Jumping the Hurdle

The object of this particular exercise is to teach the dog to jump and clear a hurdle and to remain stationary on the other side in the stand position. The ultimate aim is to send the dog forward from any distance in front of the hurdle, and after it has jumped it and remains standing, to join the dog and walk away with it at heel. The word of command is 'UP'.

Commence with the dog on your left side and on a long training lead. The size of the hurdle will depend on the breed and size of the dog, although a hurdle of about one foot (300 mm) in height is a good average size to begin with. Step over the hurdle, taking the dog with you and remember to give the command 'UP' just before the dog goes over. The speed at which you approach the hurdle will depend very much on the capabilities of the dog, and great care should be taken to make sure that you do not approach the hurdle too quickly, otherwise the dog could injure itself by trying to jump it too hurriedly. Praise the dog when it has gone over the hurdle and repeat the exercise. The dog will quickly become tired in the early stages of this training and it will therefore be necessary to give it a rest after it has gone over the hurdle four or five times. A few short sessions each day will gradually build up the dog's confidence and indeed its physical condition.

Progress to a higher hurdle when the dog is clearing the lower one without difficulty. Instead of stepping over the hurdle, you can now walk close to it and guide the dog over by means of the lead (*photo 23*). The lead should not be held in such a way that it impedes the dog's progress and it should not therefore be held tightly. Do not forget to praise the dog when it has cleared the hurdle and remember to halt with the dog in the stand position when it reaches the other side.

When the dog is clearing the hurdle without difficulty, higher hurdles can be slowly introduced until the dog is able to clear a reasonably high one. The final heigh depends on the size and physical capabilities of the dog and the common sense of the owner, but a dog such as an Alsatian can be expected to clear a minimum of three feet (0.90 m). Many smaller breeds are of course equally capable of jumping this height.

When the dog is clearing the hurdle confidently and with ease, the lead can be removed but do not be tempted to remove it too soon. The exercise off the lead should be carried out exactly as you did it with the dog on the lead. Remember to give the command 'UP' just before the dog goes over the hurdle, halt with the dog in the stand at heel position after it has gone over and walk away with the dog at heel, thus completing the exercise.

The next stage is to send the dog forward and over the hurdle rather than moving forward with it as you did in the previous exercise. It is advisable not to stand too far away from the hurdle and a suitable distance would be about five paces (*photo 24*). You will have to be guided by how agile your particular dog is, however, and whether or not it requires a good run to give it the impetus to jump the hurdle. When the dog has cleared the hurdle, you should cause it to stop in the stand position by giving the command 'STAY'. Walk forward and stand by the dog and after a pause, give the command 'HEEL' and walk away with it. It is important that you have complete control of the dog during this and all other agility exercises.

The Long Jump

This consists of a number of very low hurdles which are spaced out in such a manner as to form a long jump. The word

of command is 'OVER' and the dog should clear the jump and remain stationary on the other side as it did in the previous exercise. You can run with the dog up to the hurdles, stand in front of them and call the dog over, or send the dog forward and over. When running with the dog or calling it over, you should not go past the first hurdle yourself (*photo 25*). When the dog has remained in the stand position on command at the other side of the long jump, you should walk forward to it and after a pause walk away with it at heel to complete the exercise.

Commence by having the dog on a long training lead and by using a short jump.

24. *Dog being sent forward over the hurdle.*

39

25. *Initial stage of training in long jump.*

Again it will be necesary to take into consideration the size and breed of the dog and most of all its physical capabilities. For most of the medium-sized and larger dogs, the hurdles should be spaced out to form a jump which is about three feet (0.90 m) long, whilst with some of the smaller breeds it will need to be about half that distance. The height of the hurdles will vary from eight inches to one foot (200 to 300 mm).

With the dog on the lead run to the jump, and giving the command 'OVER', encourage it to jump the hurdles. Make sure that the lead is completely slack as a tight lead will impede the dog's progress and also cause it to jump sideways. If the dog goes over the hurdle without any trouble, give it the usual praise, cause it to stand and after a pause walk away with it at heel. If, however, the dog has difficulty in getting over the hurdles, try again, this time taking a longer run. If it again fails, shorten the length of the jump and repeat the exercise.

As the dog improves, gradually add more hurdles until finally it is able to clear a fairly long jump. This would be about nine feet (2.74 m) for the medium and larger dogs and about half that distance for the smaller breeds (*photo 26*). I would again point out that some of the small breeds are extremely agile and it must be left to the common sense of the owner to decide what length a particular dog is capable of jumping.

When the dog is jumping well on the lead and not before, the lead can be removed and the exercise repeated. Continue to run with the dog at your side and keep close to the hurdles yourself to stop the dog from jumping sideways. Place the dog in the stand position when it has gone over, stand by it for a short time and walk away with it at heel.

The stage will finally be reached when the dog is clearing the long jump off the lead with confidence and ease. Up till now you have been running with the dog at your side, but you can now try the other two methods and decide which one is the most suitable for your dog. As previously mentioned, one method is to stand in front of the hurdle and call the dog over from a distance (*photo 27*), and the other is to send the dog forward. Whether you run with the dog, call it from a distance or send it forward, you must always finish the exercise properly by stopping it in the stand position after it has done the jump, walking to the dog and after a pause walking away with it at heel. This gives a neat and tidy finish to the exercise and introduces the necessary control which is so important in all dog training.

Quite often the dog will go over the long jump, but it will be inclined to knock over some of the small hurdles which combine to form the jump. In other words, it is not jumping high enough. If this is the case, you should raise the middle hurdle by placing another one on the top of it. This will not only teach the dog to jump higher, but by jumping higher it will also increase the length of its jump.

Do not prolong the exercise until the dog becomes tired and bored. After it has gone over the jump four or five times you

26. *Second stage of training in long jump.*

41

27. *Dog being called over the long jump.*

should either give it a rest or change to another exercise.

The Scale Exercise

The scale obstacle, or scramble board as it is sometimes called, consists of a number of boards which are slotted into a solid and rigid framework to form a high obstacle. The boards are slotted into the framework in order that the overall height of the obstacle can be highered or lowered as necessary. The boards should be at least one inch (25 mm) thick and six inches (150 mm) wide, and the overall width of the obstacle at least five feet (1.50 m). The height of the obstacle when fully extended should be a minimum of six feet (1.80 m). The framework should be constructed of solid three by three-inch (76 mm) timber.

Many scaling obstacles have narrow wooden slats running along each of the boards to assist the dog in scaling. The slats can be a great help in the initial stages of training, but it is advisable to do away with them once the dog has been taught to scale. A dog which has always been assisted by slats will have difficulty in scaling ordinary boards, but a dog trained on ordinary boards will have no difficulty when assisted by slats.

It is very important that the scale obstacle is constructed in such a manner that it is rigid and secure, and for that reason the two uprights should be connected by a securing rod which can be tightened at one end.

In this exercise the dog does not clear the obstacle as it did the hurdle. Because of the excessive height, the only way the dog can get over is by jumping upwards and at the same time pushing with its hind legs and pulling itself over with its front legs. It is very important that the dog is fully fit and physically capable before you commence the training.

The ultimate aim is to be able to send the dog forward over the obstacle, to stop it in the sit, down or stand position on the other side and, after a pause, to call it back over the obstacle to the sit-in-front position. After a further pause the dog is placed in the sit-at-heel position and the exercise thus completed.

Commence the training with the dog on a long training lead and the scale obstacle fixed at about six inches (150 mm) higher than the maximum height you have taught it to jump the hurdles. With the dog at heel and about the same distance from the obstacle as it is high, quickly move forward with the dog giving the command 'UP' as it reaches the obstacle. Make sure that the lead is slack and that it does not in any way impede the dog (*photo 28*).

If the dog goes over, you should release the lead and run round to the other side of the obstacle to the dog. Praise it and repeat the exercise from that side. When the dog has gone over about four times, give it a rest or change to another exercise.

Although the general rule is to place the dog the same distance from the obstacle as the obstacle is high, it may be necessary to take a slightly longer run with the dog if it refuses to go over at first from the recognised distance. Do not take too long a run, however, or the dog may try to jump and clear the obstacle rather than scale it, and if this happens, it could either injure itself or, at the least, hit the obstacle and fall backwards. In either case it would cause the dog to be very dubious of attempting the exercise the next time.

Give the command 'UP' in a very encouraging and urgent tone of voice so that it will give the dog the added incentive to negotiate the obstacle. It may also be necessary to assist the dog by supporting its hind-quarters as it attempts to scale the obstacle. Do not try to push or force the dog over, however, as this could cause it to fall awkwardly.

Continue to work the dog on the lead, and as the scaling improves, gradually increase the height by adding one board at a time. The training must not be rushed, and after the dog has gone over four or five times it should either be rested or you should change over to another exercise. Continue also to join the dog on the other side and, after a pause, to direct it back over the obstacle to the original side where you should again join it and give it the usual praise.

28. *Teaching the dog to scale: initial stage.*

43

29. *Dog being directed over the scale obstacle off the lead.*

When the dog is really doing well and going over the obstacle confidently and with ease, the lead can be removed and the finishing touches put to the exercise.

Place the dog in the sit position at heel and the correct distance from the scale obstacle. Give the command 'UP' and send it forward and over, giving the command 'STAY' when it reaches the other side (*photo 29*). Make sure that the dog is not too close to the obstacle when you give the command 'STAY', otherwise it may be too close to the obstacle to do the return scale. After a pause give the command 'UP' and get the dog to return over the obstacle to sit in front of you. After a further pause direct the dog to the sit-at-heel position, thus completing the exercise in a neat and tidy fashion.

Although many breeds of dogs will be able to scale at least six feet (1.80 m) you will obviously have to be guided by the size, breed and physical capabilities of your own dog when deciding what the maximum scaling height will be. Some dogs will be capable of scaling considerably more than six feet, but it should be stressed that on no account should this exercise be overdone as excessive heights and continuous training could cause permanent injury and heart strain.

A quick and easy method of teaching a dog to scale is to place a heavy door or similar object at an angle in front of the scale obstacle so that it rests near to the top of it, forming a platform for the dog to run up (*photo 30*). When this method is used, the exercise is carried out exactly as

30. *Quick method of teaching the dog to scale.*

described earlier, with the dog on the lead in the initial stages. It will of course be much easier for the dog to run up and scale the door than to scale the obstacle itself.

As the dog gains in confidence, the door can be gradually pushed closer to the scale obstacle itself. It should be pushed more closely at the base so that the angle becomes more acute and finally so close as to be almost perpendicular (*photo 31*). When this stage has been reached and the dog is going over with confidence and without difficulty, the door can be discarded.

31. *Dog going over the scale obstacle with door almost perpendicular.*

The Sendaway and Redirection Exercises

The send-away and redirection exercises are two separate ones although, when the dog is fully trained in both, the two can be coupled together.

The exercises are very difficult ones to teach the dog, and complete success will never be achieved without perseverance and above all determination.

On no account must the redirection be attempted until the sendaway has been fully mastered, and in any case neither exercise must be attempted until a very good standard has been reached in all the obedience exercises so far.

The ultimate aim is to be able to send the dog away on the command 'AWAY', in a straight line to a given point. It should go away at a good speed without stopping, turning round, or deviating from the straight line in any way, and it should continue until given a further command and placed in the sit, down or stand position.

The next stage is to redirect the dog either to the left or right. The word of command is 'LEFT' if the dog is required to go to your left, and 'RIGHT' if you require it to go to the right. The signal is to extend the appropriate arm sideways. On the command and signal the dog should again move at a good speed at a right angle from you. It should not deviate in any way and it should continue until placed in the sit, down or stand position.

The exercise is completed by a recall.

Commence with the dog at heel and in the sit position. Give the command 'STAY' and walk away from the dog in a straight line for a distance of about twenty paces at first. Place out a fairly large article which is too big for the dog to retrieve. It does not matter what the article is, providing that it is sufficiently conspicuous.

Return to the dog and place it in the stand position in front of you with your legs on either side of the dog. Bend down and point in the direction of the article and at the same time give the command 'AWAY'. The dog will connect the exercise with the retrieve and it will run out towards the article (*photo 32*). Just before it reaches the article you should command it to stop in the sit, down or stand position. You may find that the down is the most effective one of the three.

After a pause you should go to the dog and praise it. On no account should you call the dog to you at this stage or indeed at any time until the sendaway and the redirection exercises have been fully mastered.

Repeat the exercise, placing the article out in different areas and gradually increasing the distance. With continued training the dog will begin to connect the command with going away rather than with the retrieve exercise and when this stage has been reached it will be possible to send the dog away without the aid of the article. Remember that you must go to the dog and not call it to you.

The exercise can be carried out by following the procedure as previously described but without the aid of an article. Instead of placing out the article, you should walk away as before, turn about and face the dog and go through the actions of placing an article on the ground.

The dog will of course connect the exercise with the retrieve at first, but after a while it will realise that there is no article there and will begin to respond to the command 'AWAY'. When this stage has been reached you should walk away for about twenty paces and return to the dog without the pretence of placing an article on the ground.

Whichever method is used for this exercise, it is important that you change

over to other parts of the training area and change the direction of the sendaway, also that you slowly increase the length of the sendaway as the training improves.

32. *Dog being sent away towards an article.*

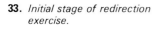

33. *Initial stage of redirection exercise.*

When it is obvious that the dog is responding to the command and is going away freely and happily in a straight line, it will no longer be necessary for you to walk out in front of it. It can now be sent away in the normal manner as described above. Much patience and determination will still be required and you will have to spend as much time as possible in order to obtain the desired standard.

There is no set distance for the sendaway exercise but a well-trained dog should have no difficulty in doing at least 100 yards (100 m).

It is emphasised that you go to the dog and do not call it at this stage. It is also very important that the dog is given much praise when it has done the exercise, even though the sendaway may only have been a short one.

One of the main problems in training for the sendaway exercise is to get the dog to go away in a straight line. This problem can be overcome to some extent by doing the exercise in an area where its movements are somewhat restricted such as an alleyway, an area between two buildings or a walled or fenced-in pathway. The dog will have no alternative but to go in a straight line and with continued training it will become accustomed to doing so. After the dog has done a few sendaways in the restricted area, you should change over to open ground and alternate between the two.

The Redirection Exercise

The object of this exercise is to be able to send the dog to the left or right when it is at a distance from you. As explained earlier, the word of command is 'LEFT' if the dog is required to move to your left,

34. *Dog being redirected in an open area.*

and 'RIGHT' if you require it to go to your right. The signal, which should be given at the same time as the command, is to extend the appropriate arm sideways.

The redirection exercise should be done as an entirely separate one and should never be done in conjunction with the sendaway at this stage. Later on, when the dog is doing well, it will be possible to couple the two exercises together, but if this is done in the early stages it will confuse the dog and therefore ruin all that you have done.

Some owners use the command 'AWAY' for both the sendaway and the redirection exercises, although they use the correct signal. It is common sense to assume that this will cause considerably confusion to the dog and that training results will suffer.

The command 'GO' is also commonly used for these exercises. It is not a satisfactory command as it can easily be mistaken for the command 'NO', particularly when the dog is working at a distance.

Commence the training for this exercise with the dog in the stand position and placed by a wall, hedge or fence so that its movements are restricted. In this position it will be able to move to the left or right but will be unable to go away from you.

Stand about ten paces away from the dog with the wall, hedge or fence in the background and, after a pause, give the command 'LEFT', extending your left arm sideways as you do so. Step sideways to your left with the arm still extended, praising the dog as it moves in the desired direction.

When the dog has gone to your left for about ten paces, give the command 'STAY' and return to it making a fuss of it.

Leave the dog in the stand position and again face it from about ten yards (9 m). This time repeat the exercise, but change the direction to your right (*photo 33*). The command of course will be 'RIGHT', and

the right arm will be extended sideways. Repeat the exercise about six times, sending the dog in alternate directions. Give the dog a rest or change to another exercise, returning to the redirection later on.

Do not continually direct the dog from left to right and vice versa. If you do this, it will begin to connect the next command with moving in the opposite direction and will anticipate the command. In other words, you should occasionally send the dog to the left, stop it and, after a pause, send it further to your left. The same will apply to the redirection right.

As the training improves, you should gradually increase the distance between yourself and the dog and the distance of the redirection. You should also refrain from taking the sideways steps, and the sooner this can be done the better.

The next stage is to do the training in an open area without the aid of the wall, fence or hedge. Before this can be done, however, you should be satisfied that a good standard has been reached in the restricted area and that the dog fully understands the command and signal and is responding accordingly (*photo 34*).

When moving to open ground, it is advisable to stand about ten paces away from the dog at first as you did at the beginning of the training, gradually increasing the distance as progress is made. Continue to return to the dog and to give it the usual praise when it has responded. Remember to change over to another exercise if the dog is showing signs of becoming bored.

If the dog does not respond when the training is done in the open, or if it does not keep at right angles to you, it will be necessary to revert to the original training in the restricted area, although this must not be continued indefinitely.

Always make sure that your commands

and signals are clear and concise as the dog can easily mistake them, particularly when it is working at a distance from you.

When the redirection exercise has been fully mastered it will be possible to do it in conjunction with the sendaway exercise as previously explained. Although the recall can also be introduced, it should only be done on occasions during the training sessions. It is advisable to go to the dog in the majority of cases and only call it occasionally.

Although the dog has been placed in the stand position during the training for this exercise, it can be placed in the sit or down position after it has been redirected.

2
Tracking

IN ITS wild state the dog had to track down other animals in order to survive and for this reason nature has given it a very acute sense of smell. This natural instinct has been developed in the trained domesticated tracker dog so that it can follow the trail of a human.

It is commonly thought that a dog is following human scent only when it is tracking. This is a misconception as the dog can be following one or more of a number of different kinds of scent.

The main scents which combine to make a track scent are: human; crushed vegetation; crushed insects and worms; disturbed earth; leather, rubber, plastic, etc. from footwear; shoe polishes and clothing.

Human Scent

Scent is continually issuing from the pores of all animals and humans. It hangs in the air, drops to the ground and clings to clothing. Each part of the body gives off a different scent and there are no two human scents which are exactly alike.

Occupational Scent

This is the scent which is carried in the clothing of persons in various kinds of employment. For example, a mechanic would leave behind the scent of oil, a cook the scent of food, and a miner the scent of coal dust.

Crushed Vegetation

When a person walks on grassland or other vegetation, the vegetation is crushed and as a result a strong scent is given off. This is probably the easiest scent for the dog to follow.

Crushed Insects

There are of course millions of insects and worms on and just below the surface of the ground. In fairly soft ground conditions they are crushed when the ground is walked upon, giving off a distinctive odour.

Disturbed Earth

On soft ground such as ploughed fields and gardens the earth is disturbed if walked upon. This gives off a fairly strong and interesting scent to a trained dog.

Leather, Rubber, Plastic, Etc. from Footwear

Small particles from materials used in footwear are left on the ground and the various scents from these will assist the dog, particularly when it is tracking on hard surfaces.

Shoe Polish

Shoe polish gives off a distinctive odour which will be left behind on most types of surfaces, thus assisting the dog to track.

Clothing

The type of clothing worn can affect the scent given off by a human. For example, the scent given off by a person wearing woollen clothing is different from that given off from clothing made of synthetic material.

Weather Conditions

Although a well-trained dog can track in adverse weather conditions, a track scent can be weakened by the elements. Heavy rain, strong winds, frost and hot dry conditions are not good for tracking, the best conditions being moist air and moist ground conditions with little or no wind.

Equipment

A tracking harness, made of leather or webbing, with a tracking line at least thirty-two feet (10 m) in length will be required (*photo 35*). The tracking line can be made of strong rope about the thickness of a normal clothes line or about half-inch (12 mm) nylon or similar webbing. It should have a loop at one end and a quick release clip at the other.

The dog should not be punished in any way when it is working a track. For example, if a dog is punished for losing scent whilst tracking, it will not be clever enough to reason that it has been punished for losing the scent but will connect the punishment with tracking generally. If this is the case, the dog will quickly lose all interest in the exercise or simply try to please you by putting its nose to the ground and taking you for a walk on the tracking line, rather than following a track scent.

Do not jerk or pull at the tracking line when the dog is tracing. Having trained the dog in obedience, and in particular the heel work on the lead where the lead has been used to check or correct the dog, the slightest jerk or pull on the tracking line will obviously have the same effect. This would cause the dog to stop tracking, lose its concentration, or if it is done often enough, cause it to lose all interest in the exercise.

35. *Tracking harness and tracking line.*

There are various ways in which a dog will indicate that it is tracking properly, and it is up to the owner to study the dog closely and watch its reactions. This is commonly known as being able to read your dog. Some dogs will hold their tails high when they are tracking well, others wag their tails excessively, whilst some will crouch down slightly as they move along the track.

There are many more ways in which the dog will indicate that it is on the correct trail, and a good handler will quickly observe the particular reactions of his or her dog. To the inexperienced, a dog may appear to give no indication at all when it is following a track, and although this type of dog may be rather difficult to read, its owner should nevertheless be quite capable of doing so.

A dog cannot concentrate on tracking if you are continually talking to it. The command 'TRACK' should only be used when the dog has lost the scent, or if it is having difficulty, and it should not be used when the dog is actually tracking. The command should be given in a quiet and encouraging tone of voice and not as a direct command as in some of the other exercises. When the dog is tracking well it should be given quiet praise from time to time to reassure it, but the praise should not be overdone.

A good tracker dog should track at a reasonably steady pace. If it tracks at a fast speed, it will be inclined to miss the turns on the track and also any articles which are on the track. It is therefore important that you do not run behind the dog and cause it to quicken its pace.

You can only teach the dog to track by doing successful tracks. If the dog fails on a track, it has been taught nothing, in fact the training has taken a backward step. It is extremely important, therefore, that if the dog fails, another track which is slightly easier is laid in order that the dog can be successful. The dog will track for two reasons: one is to please itself and the other to please you. If it fails a track, it has not pleased itself and it knows that it has not pleased you.

The way the tracking line is handled is a most important factor; perhaps a good line handler can be enlikened to a good fisherman. At no time should the line be allowed to become entangled with the dog or indeed with any obstacles which may be encountered on the track.

It often happens that a handler will think that he knows better than the dog and as a result the dog is pulled off the track when it is doing well. This is very bad handling and it should always be remembered that the dog can track and the handler cannot.

When laying a track in open fields it is bad policy to always walk through gateways, gaps and natural openings in the perimeter hedges, walls or fences. If this is done frequently, the dog will become so accustomed to going through them that it may do so even if there is no track scent there.

It will be much better if the tracklayer will climb over the various obstacles, rather than using the obvious easy way all the time.

Another bad fault in tracklaying is to always use the perimeter of a field and therefore laying the track close to the boundary fence. Use the perimeter on occasions by all means, but try to use the open area as much as possible.

Tracking Training: First Stage

The first stage in tracking training is to get the dog accustomed to wearing the tracking harness. It will be necessary to fit the harness on the dog for a few times prior to commencing the actual field work.

36. *Dog being encouraged to start a track in the initial stage of the training.*

This should be done over a period of two days, although the harness should not be left on the dog for long periods.

Make sure that the harness is fitting properly and that there is no discomfort whatsoever to the dog. When the dog is quite content to wear the harness, the first training track can be attempted.

Select a suitable area of reasonably short grassland where there is no interference from other persons, animals or vehicles. You will need an assistant to lay the track for you, although later on you will be able to lay your own tracks from time to time.

Hold the dog on the training lead whilst the assistant walks away in a straight line for a distance of about fifty yards (45 m). The assistant will then place on the ground an article with which the dog is familiar, making sure that the dog has seen him do so. He will then return to you by making a detour, keeping at least thirty yards (27 m) from his outward track. The point where the assistant has placed the article on the ground will be the end of the track as far as the training is concerned, although it is obvious that the track scent cannot end there and it will continue as long as the tracklayer continues to walk. All that is

needed at this stage of the training is to get the dog to track in a straight line to the article and not all the way round the track to the starting point.

When the track has been laid and the assistant has returned to you, you should at once fit the harness on the dog and clip the training lead to the ring on the top of the harness. At this stage the training lead is used in preference to the tracking line.

Bend down and with a sweeping movement of the right arm indicate the start of the track to the dog, at the same time giving the command 'TRACK' in a quiet but encouraging tone of voice (*photo 36*).

Having seen the article being placed by the assistant, the dog will be interested in going forward and you should walk with it, holding the lead in your right hand. The lead should not be held tightly and it should not be pulled or jerked.

After the dog has gone forward for a few yards, it will commence to use its nose to some extent and quiet praise should be given when it does so. When it reaches the article it should be praised enthusiastically and the harness removed. The article should then be thrown for the dog to

54

retrieve and again it should be given plenty of praise.

Repeat the exercise, giving the dog two or three tracks each day. It is very important that you change the area for each of the daily tracks, as the intermingling of the track scents would completely confuse the dog if the same area were used. This will apply when all future training tracks are done. After a minimum of twenty-four hours it will, however, be possible to use the area again.

As the training improves, the length of the track can be extended, and similarly the waiting period between laying the track and running it. This must be a gradual process and you will have to be guided by how well the dog is tracking. The waiting period can be increased by about five minutes at a time and the length of the track by about twenty paces. On no account should the waiting period be increased unless the dog is really doing well at a given period.

When the dog is tracking well for a distance of approximately 150 yards (137 m) on a five-minute-old scent, the tracking line can be substituted for the training lead and, in addition, the track can be laid out of sight of the dog. It will, however, be necessary for you to observe the track being laid, and you should know exactly where to start the dog on the track.

Prior to starting the track, the tracking line should be rolled up in such a manner that it can be clipped to the harness on the dog at the start of the track and thrown out behind you so that it falls to the ground in a straight line without becoming entangled.

Place the harness on the dog and fasten the clip of the line to the ring on the top of the harness. Throw the line out behind you and take hold of it near to the dog's shoulders, giving the command 'TRACK' in the usual quiet but encouraging tone of voice. As the dog moves forward you should stand still and allow the line to pass through your hand until there is about one yard (0.90 m) of the line left. At this stage you should move forward behind the dog, making sure that you do not pull or jerk the tracking line.

Give the dog quiet praise from time to time when it is doing well and only use the command when the dog is losing interest or it is not quite on the track. Give the dog praise when it finds the article at the end of the track, remove the harness and throw the article for the dog to retrieve. The harness should always be removed immediately the track is finished and it should not be fitted to the dog until the track is ready to be run.

Tracking Training: Second Stage

When the dog is tracking well on a ten minutes' old scent, articles can be placed out on the track in addition to the familiar article which is left at the end. Gradual turns can also be introduced to the track.

The articles should be well spaced out and placed on the track and not on either side of it, neither should they be placed on or near a turn. They should not be too large or conspicuous and should be fairly well handled so that they bear a human scent.

The shape of the articles does not matter and they may be made of cloth, rubber, leather, plastic, wood or metal. A suitable size at this stage of the training would be something about the size of a matchbox, but later on, as the training improves, much smaller articles can be used. Three articles will be sufficient at first, but after a while a few more may be used as the length of the track is gradually increased.

The placing of the articles will have a beneficial effect on the dog's tracking capabilities as it will induce the dog to keep its nose to the ground.

37. *Dog going down on finding an article on the track.*

The turns which have now been introduced into the track pattern, should be gradual ones, and the track layer should return to the start of the track as before, by means of a detour, after the familiar article has been placed out to indicate the end of the track.

As soon as the dog finds an article on the track, you should place the animal in the down position, drop the tracking line on the line of the track and run to the dog giving it the usual praise as you do so. After taking the article from it you should take hold of the tracking line near to the dog's shoulders, give the command 'TRACK' and allow the line to pass through your hand as the dog moves forward, just as you did at the beginning of the track. Eventually, with continued training, the dog will go down on its own accord when it finds an article (*photo 37*).

It should be pointed out at this stage that the reason the dog is placed in the down position is because it is the most positive way it will be able to indicate that it has found the article. Quite often a dog

which has not been taught to go down at an article will pick it up, carry it for a short distance and then drop it, unnoticed by the handler. A dog which goes down by an article when tracking during the hours of darkness will also give a positive indication, and, in addition, damage to the articles by chewing and mouthing will be eliminated.

At this stage of the training you should observe the track being laid, making sure that you are familiar with its shape. In this way you will be in a position to assist the dog if it is having difficulty at a particular point on the track. It is emphasised that the dog should only be assisted as a very last resort, after it has been allowed to search for the scent without success.

When assisting the dog, great care should be taken not to jerk or pull the dog onto the track, otherwise it will eventually expect to be assisted whenever it is having difficulty and will respond to the slightest jerk on the tracking line.

Once the dog is tracking efficiently and confidently over the various types of terrain

56

it will no longer be necessary for you to know the shape of the track. From time to time you may lay your own tracks, particularly when you are unable to obtain the assistance of another person. It is far better to lay a track yourself than not to do a training track at all.

Tracking Training: Third Stage

With continued training the dog's tracking capabilities will improve and it will eventually begin to connect the sight of the tracking harness with the tracking exercise. A keen tracker dog will become quite excited as soon as the harness is produced.

When the dog is doing well on a scent which is twenty minutes old and is indicating the articles, it will be time to introduce right-angle turns into the track pattern. The turns should be at least fifty paces apart and, as previously stated, articles should not be placed on or near a turn.

About two turns will be sufficient at first, but as the training improves one or two more can be introduced. The tracklayer will continue to make a detour after placing out the familiar article. and it will still be necessary for you to watch the track being laid. As before, you will be able to lay the track yourself from time to time.

If the dog is having a little difficulty on a turn, you should allow it to work for and find the scent itself and not be tempted to assist it in any way. If, however, it is having considerable difficulty and becoming tired or frustrated, then you should gently guide it onto the turn giving it plenty of praise as soon as it picks up the scent.

When laying a track yourself, it is advisable to get someone else to handle the articles which you will be placing on the track. The articles can be placed in a small receptacle of some kind after they have been well handled by another person and you can place them on the track without having to handle them.

The continued use of articles which bear your own scent would eventually cause the dog to discriminate and it would therefore only show interest in articles which you have handled.

Continue to increase the waiting period between laying and running the tracks and, in addition, the length of the tracks, but do not increase either the waiting period or the length of the track unless the dog is tracking well on a particular age of track scent. When the dog is tracking well at a 30-minute-old scent, it will be possible to increase the waiting period by fifteen minutes at a time instead of the five minutes.

Tracking Training: Fourth Stage

When the dog is tracking well on an hour-old scent, the track can be laid out of your sight so that you have no knowledge of its shape. You will need to be told where the track will commence but not the direction taken by the tracklayer.

Up till now you have been able to see the track laid or, alternatively, you have laid it yourself, and because of this you have been able to watch the dog's reactions on turns and the various types of terrain. In other words, you have learned to read your dog much better than you would have done had you not been familiar with the shape of the track. You have also been in a position to assist the dog if necessary and, as a result, you have been able to make the training successful. None of this would have been possible if you had not known the shape and layout of the track, and quite obviously many mistakes would have been made by yourself and the dog.

Although you will know where the track will commence, you will not know the direction taken by the tracklayer and it will therefore be necessary to allow the dog to cast around at the start in order to pick up the track scent.

After fitting the harness and attaching the tracking line in the correct manner, take hold of the line in about the centre and give the command 'TRACK', allowing the dog to search for the scent. As soon as the dog gives a positive indication, you should move forward and allow the line to pass through your hand until there is only the usual one yard (0.90 m) left.

If the dog has difficulty at a given point on the track, you should stand still and allow it to cast around and regain the track scent. Hold the tracking line fairly high so that the line does not become entangled with the dog, and be extremely careful not to pull or jerk at the line. As soon as the dog gives a positive indication that it has found the scent, you should move forward giving it the usual quiet but necessary praise.

It may be that the dog will still be unable to regain the track scent even though it has worked hard in an effort to do so. If this is the case, you should take the dog back to a point on the track where it was tracking well and restart the track from there. It usually happens that it will then continue to follow the scent over the area where it was previously having difficulty.

Due to various reasons, such as interference from people and animals having walked over the track, the change in ground conditions, or exposure to high winds, etc., the dog may continue to have difficulty when it reaches the particular point on the track. If so, you should take it forward for a few yards and try again, and if this is not successful, try to restart the dog a few yards to the left and alternatively to the right.

If the dog fails the track, then you

38. *Dog searching for the track scent at the start of a track.*

should arrange for a slightly easier track to be laid, making sure that the dog is successful.

It is not necessary for all training tracks to be laid out of your view, and you may in fact continue to lay them yourself occasionally. It must be emphasised, however, that some of the tracks must be laid completely out of your view and that you have no knowledge of their shape. You will obviously have to know roughly where the track begins, although it is advisable to allow the dog to search for the start in an area of about fifteen feet by fifteen feet (4.5 m x 4.5 m) rather than putting it directly onto the track at the start of it (*photo 38*). The area from which the track will start can be marked out if necessary.

Try to give the dog at least two successful tracks each week and remember that they must be successful, otherwise you will be wasting your time. With correct and sensible training the dog will eventually be capable of following a scent which is many hours old.

Tracking: Incentive Method

It sometimes happens that a dog shows little or no interest in the tracking exercise in the early stages of training. If this is so, it is very frustrating to the owner, particularly when the dog stands still and refuses even to attempt to follow the trail.

If your dog is like this, other methods will have to be used to give the dog the necessary incentive to track.

One method is to lay the track yourself, whilst an assistant holds your dog at the start of the track. The dog will see you walk away and naturally it will want to follow you. Lay a straight track of about two hundred yards (182 m) and instead of dropping an article and returning by means of a detour to the start, you should conceal yourself at the end of the track.

When you are out of sight, the assistant will place the harness on the dog and after clipping on the tracking line, he will handle the dog on the track.

In all probability, the dog will run forward with its head in the air for the first few yards, but it should quickly settle down and put its nose to the ground when it realises that it is following your trail. Both the assistant and yourself should praise the dog when it finds you.

Although this is a very good method of giving the dog the incentive to track, it is not advisable to do too many in this way. In any case, two or three tracks laid and run in this manner will probably be sufficient to give the dog the necessary interest in following a track, and the ordinary training methods can be reverted to.

Another method which can be used to give the dog the necessary incentive to follow a track is a rather old-fashioned one, but nevertheless one which has proved over the years to be very effective.

In order to train your dog by this method, it will be necessary for you to be accompanied by at least one other handler and dog, although three or four would be the ideal number. It will also be a great advantage if your dog is familiar with the handlers and their dogs.

The idea is for the other handlers and dogs to walk away from you in single file and after walking for about two hundred yards (182 m), to conceal themselves. This can be done by hiding behind a wall, in trees and bushes, or even in a hollow in the ground. Naturally you will have selected a suitable area of grassland which can be utilised for this purpose.

Your dog should be able to watch the rest walk away but it should not be able to see exactly where they have gone or where they have hidden. Because your dog has been left behind, it will become rather excited and naturally it will want to join its friends; for this reason it will show a keen interest in following their trail.

When the group have been out of sight for about three or four minutes, you should place the tracking harness on the dog, attach the line and commence the track in the normal way. The added incentive to track will cause the dog to work much harder than it has done hitherto, and although it may be inclined to put its head in the air from time to time in an effort to air-scent the other dogs, it will also show a keen interest in the track scent.

When the dog has tracked to the other handlers and dogs, it should not be allowed to actually come in contact with the other dogs as they may resent its sudden intrusion and a fight could ensure. This could have an adverse effect on the dog and cause it to lose further interest in the tracking. You should of course praise the dog when it has completed the track, and the other handlers should do likewise.

I should point out that this method is purely an incentive method in tracking training, and because of the nature of the track scent, it would be most unwise to overdo it. It is a very good method to stimulate the dog's interest in tracking, but not more than two or three tracks should be done in this way. This should be sufficient to create the necessary interest, and you can revert to the ordinary training methods as described earlier.

Free Tracking

Free tracking is nothing more than a long distance retrieve, but it is a very important and valuable exercise which will improve the leash or line tracking training.

As much free tracking as possible should be done, providing, as always, that the dog does not become tired or bored.

Select a suitable area of open grassland for the free tracking training, and as in the leash or line tracking, you should not use the same ground twice in one day.

Lay the track exactly as you would lay a leash or line track, but the only article to be placed on the track will be an article at the end. This should be a familiar article to the dog and one that it is extremely interested in.

You will have to be guided by how well the dog is working when deciding what shape and what length the free tracks will be.

After laying the track and returning to the dog by means of a detour, send the dog to fetch the article just as you would with an ordinary retrieve exercise but this time use the command 'TRACK AND FETCH' instead of the single command 'FETCH'.

3
Searching

Searching for Property

THIS EXERCISE is similar to the retrieve except that the dog is expected to find and retrieve the articles by using its sense of smell rather than its eyesight. The dog should systematically search a given area for any articles which have been handled and therefore bear a human scent.

When the dog has been successful in finding and retrieving an article, it is redirected into the area to search for any further articles which may be there. The owner should remain outside the area whilst the dog is searching, but although the dog is working free it should be under verbal control at all times. It is important that the dog has reached a good standard in the retrieve exercise before the searching training is attempted.

In working trials, the area is usually marked out to form a square by means of four marker pegs (*photo 39*). The handler is allowed to take up any position outside the area and to walk round the perimeter, but he will not be allowed to enter the area

39. *Trained dog searching a marked-out area in police-dog trials.*

itself. The size of the area may vary but it is usually not more than twenty-five yards square (21 m²).

Commence the training by selecting an area of fairly long grass or other vegetation. Place out a well-handled article about ten paces away from the dog, and after returning to the dog, give the command 'FETCH' just as you did in the retrieve exercise. Because the article is hidden in the long vegetation, it will be necessary for the dog to use its scenting powers to find it rather than its eyesight, and when the animal commences to search quiet encouragement should be given.

It will greatly assist the dog if it is sent into the area against the wind so that the scent of the article is blown towards it. It should be praised when it has located the article and again when it has delivered the article to you. At this stage of the training the article may be anything with which the dog is familiar but it should not be so large that it can be seen easily.

The next stage is to deposit an article without the dog having seen you do so. Follow the procedure as above and remember to give it quiet verbal encouragement and praise when it is successful. Because the dog has not seen the article being placed in the area, it may be reluctant to go into the area; if this is so, you should walk forward with the dog, giving it plenty of encouragement and, if necessary, help it to find the article. Even though you may have assisted the dog, it should be praised enthusiastically when it picks up the article.

When the dog is responding to the command, even though it has not seen you place out an article, two articles can be placed in the area. Immediately the dog has found one of them and delivered it to you, it should be sent in again to search for the second one. Again, if it is reluctant to go into the area to search for the second

article, you should go in with the dog and give it as much assistance as possible.

As the training improves, you should gradually increase the number of articles, so that eventually the dog will search for and find at least half a dozen articles which have been handled for a few minutes and thrown or placed into a given area. The articles may be made of wood, leather, rubber, cloth, plastic or metal, but they should not include anything made of glass or anything which could cause injury to the dog.

During the early stages of training the articles could be about the size of a matchbox but later on something much smaller could be used.

If the dog is having difficulty in finding the articles, it will quickly lose interest in the exercise; because of this it is very important that a sufficient number of articles are placed in the area. For example, if only one or two articles have been thrown or placed in an area which is twenty-five yards square (21 m²), the dog may have difficulty locating them and will become tired and frustrated. If, however, about half a dozen articles are put there, the success rate will obviously be much higher. As a result the dog will be in a much happier frame of mind and keener to work.

It is important to remember that training in this type of exercise will only improve if the dog is successful. In other words, if the dog fails to find any of the articles, the training has taken a step backwards.

When the dog is doing fairly well, it will be necessary to obtain the services of other persons who will handle the articles before they are placed in the area. If you continue to use articles which you have handled yourself, the dog will begin to discriminate and will only find the articles which you have handled. Whenever possible you should get someone to handle the articles and place them in the area, but if this cannot be arranged the articles should be handled for a few minutes by one or more persons, placed by them in a plastic bag or other similar container, and finally dropped by you in the area. The articles should be dropped directly from the bag or container; on no account should you handle them.

Whilst the dog is searching, it should be quietly encouraged and, as previously stated, the usual praise given when it finds the article. Do not continually nag at the dog or give it excessive commands, as it will not be able to concentrate on the exercise if you do.

One of the difficulties with this exercise is to keep the dog in the area to be searched. Obviously, the dog will not know when it is out of the area and will therefore need to be kept there by words of command.

To direct a dog back into an area, the command 'BACK' should be used so that the dog will turn about when the command is given. This command can be taught by giving the command every time the dog makes a natural turn so that eventually it connects the command with the movement and responds accordingly.

Many owners make the mistake of giving the command 'NO' when the dog leaves a given area. This is extremely bad practice as this command simply means that the dog should refrain from doing something contrary to its owner's wishes. In this case the dog will be searching, and by giving the command 'NO', it is being told to refrain from doing so. The dog does not have a human brain and will not be clever enough to know that it is out of an imaginary area.

Another handling fault, particularly in trials work, is for the handler to stand on the edge of the marked-out area. Quite often the articles are placed near to the edge of the area, and if the handler is standing too close, the dog will be inclined to run over the article and miss it. When a dog is being directed into an area to search, it runs with its head in the air for the first yard or so before settling down. It is always best, therefore, to stand a yard or so away from the edge of the square or area so that the dog will have its nose to the ground by the time it reaches the search area.

Searching for an Irretrievable Article

In this exercise the dog should search for and find any article which bears human scent but is too large to be retrieved. On finding the article, the dog should bark and thus indicate to its handler that it has located the article. The word of command is 'FETCH'.

Commence the training by handling a large article such as a piece of stone, metal or concrete and placing it in the training area about ten paces or so from the dog. Allow the dog to see you placing the article, return to the dog, and with it on the training lead, give the command 'FETCH'. Hold the dog on the full length of the lead and run with it to the article (*photo 40*).

At first the dog will probably try to retrieve the article but after a little while it will become frustrated and commence to whine or bark. As soon as it does this, you should praise it and encourage it to bark further. If, however, the dog is reluctant to bark, it can be encouraged to do so by giving the command 'SPEAK'.

When the dog has shown interest and barked at the article, you should pick up the article and return with the dog to your original position.

Repeat the exercise a few times, and if the dog is still reluctant to bark but prefers that you praise the dog when it finds the article and also when it commences to bark.

As the training progresses, the article can be placed in long grass or in a position out of the dog's sight so that it has to search for the scent as it did in the search for articles exercise. Ask other people to handle the article so that the dog does not become accustomed to searching for your scent only.

The ultimate aim is to be able to send the dog away from you to search a given area. On finding the irretrievable article, the dog should bark clearly on its own accord and remain with it until you join it.

Searching for a Hidden Person

The object of this exercise is for the dog to search a building, or an outside area such as woodland, for anyone who may be hiding. The dog is turned loose and should bark clearly on finding the hidden person, even though the person may be out of the animal's sight. In this case the dog will bark on finding a scent given off by the person concealed. On finding him, the dog should remain with him and continue to bark until the handler arrives. It should not attack or become too aggressive but should keep the person under surveillance. The word of command is 'FIND HIM'.

Commence by selecting a suitable wooded area where an assistant may conceal himself. With the dog on the training lead, give the command 'FIND HIM' in an encouraging tone of voice and walk into the area towards the hidden person and against the wind direction. His body scent will be blown towards the dog and as soon as it gives a positive indication that it has picked up the scent, it should be encouraged to move forward towards him and further encouraged to bark when it actually finds him. The command

40. *Initial stage in the search for an irretrievable article.*

to bite at it and attempt to retrieve it, it can be induced to bark by holding it on the lead about a yard (0.90 m) from the article. Because it cannot reach the article, it will bark out of excitement and frustration and should be fully praised when it does so.

The next stage is to place out the article, and after giving the command 'FETCH', allow the dog to run to it on its own accord. Do not give the command 'SPEAK' if it barks on reaching the article, as the object of the exercise is to get it to bark without being told to do so. If it is still reluctant to bark, then of course it must be encouraged as much as possible and given the command 'SPEAK'. It is important

'SPEAK' may be used in the initial stages, and the dog should be praised enthusiastically when it barks. It should remain about two paces from the assistant and on no account should it attempt to attack (*photo 41*).

Repeat the exercise, using different parts of the area each time, and after the dog has done the exercise about four times, give it a rest or change to one of the other exercises you have done so far.

When the dog is doing well on the lead, it can be sent into the area on its own accord. You should give it lots of encouragement from a distance, and as soon as it finds the assistant and commences to bark, it should be given the usual praise. Do not call the dog to you but go to it, give it further praise, search the assistant and escort him away from the area. If the dog has found the assistant but has failed to bark, then of course it must be encouraged to do so by using the command 'SPEAK'. It can also be induced to bark by the assistant teasing it but care should be taken not to overdo this, causing the dog to bite.

The next stage is to have the assistant

41. *Initial stage in the search for a hidden person.*

42. *Dog locating partly hidden criminal.*

hiding in a building. If possible, the building should be a fairly large one so that the dog will have to use its scenting powers and quarter the building in order to find him.

The assistant should position himself behind a door so that the dog is unable to see him, but at the same time is able to pick up his body scent through the gaps around the door.

With the dog on the training lead, take it into the building after giving the command 'FIND HIM'. Allow it to enter the various rooms before it actually enters the room in which the assistant is hiding and try to get it as excited as possible, treating the whole exercise as a big game.

As soon as the dog gives an indication that it has picked up the assistant's scent, you should encourage it to bark as you did on the outside search. Do not use the command 'SPEAK' if the dog barks on its own accord, and remember to give it the usual praise when it does so. Complete the exercise by escorting the assistant out of the building.

Continue the training, using different parts of the building each time. When the dog is showing a keen interest in the exercise, it can be sent into the building on its own accord whilst you remain at the entrance. Although the dog is working away from you, you should give it plenty of vocal encouragement whilst it is searching. When the dog begins to bark and give a positive indication that it has found the assistant, you should go to it, give it the usual praise and finish the exercise as previously described.

It is very important that you go to the dog when it has been successful in finding the hidden person. The dog should remain with the hidden person and continue to bark until you arrive (*photo 42*). If you call the dog away from him it will eventually return to you on its own accord, thus defeating the object of the exercise.

As the training improves, other hiding places should be selected, and you should use other assistants from time to time. On occasions an assistant should conceal himself above ground level so that the dog will not become accustomed to searching ground level only.

Later on it will be possible to have the assistant standing in the corner of a room or in a position where he is only partially concealed. Try to use as many different areas and buildings as possible and always make sure that no other persons or animals are in the area or building to be searched.

Do not scold or punish the dog if it refuses to bark on finding the assistant. It will not be clever enough to know that it is being punished for failing to bark and will therefore lose interest in the exercise generally.

4
Criminal Work

THE TRAINING in the criminal work exercises is intended mainly for those who enter or intend to enter the various working trials, dog training clubs and societies, and the handlers and trainers of dogs which are used for guard and security work.

Because of the dog's natural instinct, it is usually an easy matter to teach a dog to do criminal work but it is not quite so easy to control it. It is extremely important, therefore, that no criminal work training should be attempted unless the obedience exercises have been fully mastered, the dog is completely controllable, and you yourself have a very sound knowledge of all that is required.

The Chase and Attack

Here the object is to teach the dog to go after a fleeing criminal, to grasp him by the right arm and to hold him until the handler arrives and gives the command 'LEAVE'. The dog should leave immediately it is told to do so, and should bark and keep the criminal under strict surveillance whilst he is being searched. Whilst the search is taking place, he should be positioned between the dog and the handler so that if he attempts to get away the dog will be in a position to again chase and attack him. The word of command is 'GET HIM'.

When the criminal has been searched, the handler will call his dog to heel; it will then walk to heel on his left side whilst the criminal is escorted away about four paces in front. The dog should be extremely alert and should keep a watchful eye on the criminal during the escort in case he should decide to break away.

Commence the training by waving a piece of sacking in front of the dog. Give the command 'GET HIM' and allow the dog to grasp the sacking (*photo 43*). When it has obtained a firm hold, pull slightly against the dog but eventually ease off the pressure and allow it to pull you forward. Finally, release the pressure altogether, give the command 'LEAVE' in a very firm and commanding tone of voice and cause the dog to let go of the sacking. After it has done this for three or four times, give it a rest.

The next stage is to have the dog on the training lead whilst an assistant holds the sacking and carries out the procedure as previously described. You should keep hold of the lead and remember to give the command 'GET HIM' when you want the dog to take hold of the sacking, and 'LEAVE' when you require it to let go.

If the dog is rather reluctant to take

hold of the sacking, it will be necessary for you to revert to holding it yourself and then try to encourage the dog to hold it by treating the whole thing as a game, giving lots of encouragement and of course praise when the animal finally takes hold. As soon as the dog holds the sacking in a firm and determined manner when it is held by an assistant, the next stage, can be attempted.

The sacking should now be wrapped round the assistant's right arm so as to protect him, but about one foot (300 mm) of the material should be left hanging loose. With the dog on the lead, carry out the procedure as before, giving the correct command and the necessary praise. When the dog responds by grasping the loose end, this can be gradually reduced until the whole of the sacking is completely

round the arm. The assistant should bend the arm and 'feed' it to the dog to ensure that it will grasp the forearm and not the upper arm or shoulder. The dog will still be on the lead at this stage.

When the dog is showing a keen interest and taking a firm hold, the actual chase and attack can be attempted.

The dog should be sitting at heel and on the lead as the assistant commences to run away. You should call to the assistant to stand still or otherwise you will send the dog, at the same time keeping the dog in the sit-at-heel position. On no account should the dog be allowed to leave your side until it is told to do so.

When the assistant is about fifteen paces away and still running, you should give the command 'GET HIM' and immediately run with the dog, holding the full length of

43. *Dog being encouraged to grasp and hold a length of sacking.*

the lead in your right hand. The assistant should keep his right arm bent and feed it to the dog as it comes in to attack the arm. He should pull away slightly to cause it to hold onto the arm, and once he is satisfied that it has taken a firm hold, he should relax and allow you to call the dog off on the command 'LEAVE'. The dog should then be placed in the down position about three paces from the assistant and facing him.

Whilst the assistant is being searched, he should be positioned between yourself and the dog, and the dog should be encouraged to bark. When the search has been completed, you should call it to heel and escort the assistant away, keeping about four paces behind him as you do so (*photo 44*). After three chases you should give the dog a rest.

As the dog gains in confidence during this type of training, its bite will become harder and it will be necessary for the assistant to use a leather or strong canvas arm shield instead of the sacking only (*photo 45*). When this stage has been reached, the sacking should be tied round the arm shield but it should not be too bulky. The exercise should be carried out as before, with the dog still on the training lead.

44. *Escorting the acting criminal after the chase and attack.*

When the dog is biting cleanly and firmly and letting go of the arm immediately it is ordered to do so, the exercise should be repeated, but this time with the dog off the lead.

It is important that the dog remains

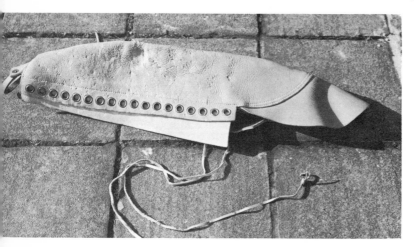

45. *The protective arm shield.*

sitting by your side as the assistant runs away and that it does not attempt to chase until it is ordered to do so. Much firmness will therefore be required. When the assistant is about twenty paces away, you should give the command 'GET HIM' and allow the dog to give chase.

When you are satisfied that it has obtained a firm hold of the right arm you should run to the dog, give the command 'LEAVE' in a commanding tone of voice and after it has released its hold, put it in the down position about three paces from the assistant.

The assistant should be between yourself and the dog whilst you search him, and finally he should be escorted away as described earlier. The dog should be encouraged to bark whilst it is guarding the assistant and whilst he is being searched.

With continued training, the stage will be reached when the assistant can wear an old coat in order to cover the protective arm shield and the sacking can be completely done away with. Because of the change from the sacking to a coat, the dog may be a little reluctant to take a firm hold of the right arm at first, but after a little while it will hold the arm equally as firmly as it did before (*photo 46*).

When the dog has reached a good standard and it is biting firmly and cleanly without too much aggression, providing you have full control of the dog, there will be no need to carry out the training continually as you do in other exercises.

The more training that is done, the harder the dog will bite and you will begin to lose some of the control which is vitally necessary in this exercise. A dog of this kind is generally known to be 'chase happy'.

Many handlers ruin excellently trained dogs by continually trying out this rather spectacular exercise. Once a good standard

46. *The chase and attack.*

has been reached, about one chase and attack every six months would be sufficient, unless of course some problem had arisen such as the dog refusing to chase or to grasp the arm.

If a trained dog suddenly refuses to chase or attack, it is possible that it has some physical defect, such as a bad tooth, a sore mouth, throat infection or ear trouble. Pain in other parts of the body could equally affect the dog when it is required to chase and attack.

It sometimes happens that the handler is entirely to blame when a dog, which hitherto has reached a good standard, suddenly becomes reluctant to chase and attack. This is when too much physical correction is used by the handler when training for this and other criminal work exercises. It can also be caused by a poor assistant who creates confusion in the

71

dog's mind so that it is unable to distinguish between this and the next training exercise, which is called the stand-off exercise.

The correct way for the assistant to run away from the dog is with his forearm bent and held about waist high. This will cause the dog to jump slightly in order to grasp the arm; as a result it will obtain a much firmer hold than it would if the arm was held low. If the arm is held low, the dog will be inclined to take hold and run alongside the assistant.

The Stand-off Exercise

This exercise involves sending the dog in pursuit of a fleeing criminal (as in the chase and attack exercise), but in this case, when the criminal stands still, the dog will refrain from attacking him.

Commence by having the dog sitting at heel and off the lead whilst the assistant commences to run away. Call to the assistant to stand still or otherwise you will release the dog, but on no account must the dog be allowed to move until it is told to do so. The assistant continues to run and when he is about fifteen paces away, you should give the command 'GET HIM', as you did in the previous exercise, and send the dog.

Immediately the dog is released, the assistant should stand still and you should give the command 'LEAVE' in a very firm and commanding voice. Run to the dog, and if it has refrained from attacking the assistant, give it the usual praise. If it has attacked the assistant, it should be severely scolded and caused to release its hold.

It is emphasised that at all times during the training for this exercise, the assistant should stand perfectly still once he has come to a halt (*photo 47*). Any movement

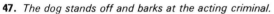

47. *The dog stands off and barks at the acting criminal.*

will cause the dog to confuse this exercise with the chase and attack, and as a result both exercises will suffer.

Repeat the exercise three or four times and then give the dog a rest.

As the training improves, the distance of the run by the assistant can be increased, and the dog can be held at your side for a longer period. The assistant can continue to run whilst the dog is in pursuit, gradually allowing the dog to get closer before standing still. During the training for this exercise do not use the command 'LEAVE' if it is obvious that the dog is not going to attack, as the object is to teach the dog to stand off or circle without any word of command. If the dog stands off or circles on its own accord, simply go to it, praise it, and complete the exercise as you did in the chase and attack.

Most dogs are reluctant to stand off or circle and they would much prefer to bite the assistant's arm. This is not because they are vicious or aggressive but because it is part of their natural instinct. The majority of trained dogs treat the chase and stand-off exercises as a big game and will chase and attack someone they know just as keenly as they would a complete stranger.

To correct a dog which is reluctant to stand off or circle, the line method can be used. A long line such as a tracking line is attached to the check chain, and the end held firmly as you send the dog. The assistant should stand still just before the dog reaches him and at the same time you should jerk the line to stop the dog from attacking. Remember to give the command 'LEAVE'.

Another method is for someone to throw a fairly heavy chain to fall close to the dog just before the assistant has stood still and before the dog has time to attack. The rattle of the chain is usually sufficient to distract the dog and stop it from attacking. The command 'LEAVE' should be given in a very determined manner just as the chain reaches the dog.

A small wire mesh compound just large enough for a person to stand inside is useful for this training. The door of the compound should have a piece of rope attached to the inside so that it can be pulled to and held by the person inside.

The assistant should run towards the compound, and the dog should be sent in pursuit, but before the dog reaches him he should enter the compound, pull the door to behind him and stand perfectly still inside.

This method will not only assist the stand-off training, but also cause the dog to circle and bark.

The Attack Under Gunfire

This exercise is similar to the ordinary chase and attack, except that the person acting as the criminal will fire a gun as the dog approaches. The most suitable type of weapon is either a .38 or .45 revolver and, naturally, the ammunition must be blank.

The exercise should not be attempted until the chase and attack has been fully mastered, although it is important that the dog is introduced to gunfire before training proper begins.

To introduce the dog to gunfire, the handler should have the dog on the lead whilst an assistant fires the revolver about one hundred yards (91 m) away. Two shots will be sufficient.

It should be pointed out at this stage that a dog can be made to be gun-shy by suddenly firing a revolver or other weapon extremely close to it.

If the dog does not show any undue apprehension when the two shots are fired, there should be no problem when the attack under gunfire exercise is commenced. If, however, the dog puts its tail between its legs, trembles with fear and

48. *Dog attacking under gunfire. Note the bent arm position of the assistant.*

The assistant should run in the usual way with the revolver in his right hand and the forearm bent (*photo 48*). If the arm is held straight and low to the ground, the dog will not get a firm grip as it will not be putting its full weight behind the attack.

The assistant should fire one round of ammunition only during each of the first few gun chases and this should be done when the dog is at least fifteen yards (14 m) away. As the dog becomes more interested in the exercise and shows no fear of the report, the number of rounds fired can be gradually increased.

Eventually the dog will become completely oblivious of the report from the weapon, and when this stage has been reached it will attack even when the asistant is standing still, providing of course that the weapon is fired before the dog is sent in.

Great care should always be taken not to fire the revolver or other weapon too close to the dog, otherwise its hearing could be affected and its eyes injured by the flames and powder burns.

As in the ordinary chase and attack training, the acting criminal should be searched and escorted away with the dog keeping him under strict surveillance at all times.

If too much training is done in this exercise, the dog will become gun-happy and you will lose the control which is so necessary. Once the exercise has been fully mastered, one chase under gunfire every six months will be quite sufficient.

Attack on Criminal Armed with a Stick or Other Weapon

This exercise is similar to the previous one except that the assistant is armed with a stick or similar weapon rather than a firearm. The dog should attack the assist-

tries to get away in any direction, it is fairly certain that it is gun-shy and there is very little that can be done to rectify the matter.

On the other hand, the sudden noise from the firing of the revolver or any other type of weapon could cause the dog to be slightly startled and to some extent this can be expected with most dogs. This slight nervousness can be overcome with training, and it should not cause too much of a problem.

Your dog has been trained to do the chase and attack exercise, so keep it at your side whilst the assistant commences to run away and until you give the command 'GET HIM'. The assistant should wear the usual protective arm shield covered by an old coat.

ant and grasp the right arm, even though it is being threatened in a very aggressive and determined manner. Although the dog should show no fear whatsoever in the face of an armed criminal, it should always be kept under strict control.

Commence with the dog off the lead and in the heel position whilst the assistant runs away brandishing a stick. On the command 'GET HIM' the dog should be sent after the assistant. Although he threatens the dog with the stick, it should grasp his right arm and hold him until the command 'LEAVE' is given (*photo 49*). At this stage the threats with the stick should be of rather a mild nature, but they should become more determined as the training progresses.

After a while, there will be no need for the assistant to run away, as the dog will attack and disarm him even when he is standing still. It is emphasised that the dog must be completely under control and that it should not under any circumstances be allowed to attack unless commanded and unless it is being threatened with a weapon.

49. *The dog disarms a man armed with a stick.*

5
Training for Demonstration Purposes

NOT EVERYONE will wish to train their dog for demonstration purposes, but for those who do, I hope the following exercises will be of some interest and help. Do not attempt the demonstration exercises, however, until your dog is doing well on all the exercises so far described.

50. *The dog goes through a hoop placed behind a hurdle.*

The Fire Hoop

The fire hoop can be quite effective and indeed spectacular. There will be no danger to the dog if common sense is used and the exercise is carried out properly.

The hoop should of course be made of metal. One-inch (25 mm) tubular steel would be sufficient for the hoop, with the upright and base about two inches (50 mm) in diameter. You will have to be guided by the breed and size of your dog, and of course how high it can jump, when deciding how high the fire hoop should be. For the medium and larger breeds the height would be about three feet (0.90 m). The diameter of the hoop should be about eighteen inches (460 mm) but it can of course be much larger if necessary. It should be constructed so that the base is solid and can not be easily knocked over.

Commence the training by teaching the dog to jump through the hoop without any fire. Place the hoop behind and close to a hurdle you have been using for the agility training, and giving the command 'UP', send the dog over the hurdle and through the hoop. Although the dog will notice the hoop, it will go through it in most cases without any trouble, simply because it is familiar with the hurdle and it has been trained to jump it (*photo 50*).

76

51. *Assistant holding the hoop.*

When the dog has gone over the hurdle and through the hoop a few times, you should take the hoop away from the hurdle and attempt to get the dog to jump through without the aid of the hurdle. In all probability it will go through without any difficulty, but if any problems are encountered, then you should revert to placing the hoop behind a hurdle.

If, however, the dog is still a little apprehensive when the hoop is away from the hurdle, you should get an assistant to hold the hoop on one side so that it is in effect much lower than when it is held upright (*photo 51*). With the dog on the training lead to give it confidence, put it through the lowered hoop and give it the usual praise. As the dog gains in confidence, the assistant should gradually higher the hoop until it is finally upright.

When the dog is finally going through the hoop off the lead with confidence and ease, you should attach a small piece of cloth to the top centre of the hoop by means of a small length of pliable wire. Make sure that the ends of the wire are not protruding in any way and that the cloth is completely secure. Pour a small amount of petrol on the cloth and light it. At this stage the flame should be little more than that of a candle flame.

Put the dog through the hoop a few times, praise it each time and give it the usual rest. Repeat the exercise later on and gradually increase the size of the cloth and the resulting flame. This build-up must be done slowly and gradually and you should not be in any hurry to put the dog through a large flame. However, once the dog is going through the fire hoop with confidence and showing no fear of the flame, the hoop can be bound by cloth on three sides, leaving the bottom free (*photo 52*). Pour the petrol on the cloth but do not overdo it at first.

To save the trouble of having to wrap

jumping through. Be extremely careful when there is a strong wind blowing, and in any case put the dog through the hoop with the wind direction and not against it, so that the flames will blow away from the dog.

The Fire Bell

It is quite an easy matter to train a dog to ring a fire bell, particularly if it is keen on the retrieve exercise. I first had the idea of getting a dog to do this many years ago and I have used it on many hundreds of demonstrations in conjunction with the fire hoop exercise.

The fire bell should be a fairly substantial one, mounted on a solid stand or framework. It should be constructed so that it can not be pulled over when the dog is ringing it by the rope.

First of all, tie a retrieve article to the end of the bell rope. Any article will do such as a piece of wood or cloth.

Give the command 'FETCH' and as soon as the dog picks up the article, give it much encouragement so that it tries to carry the article to you. By pulling at the article on the end of the rope, the dog will cause the bell to ring (*photo 53*); when this happens you should further encourage the dog and of course praise it.

With continued training the dog will begin to treat the exercise as a game, and you will have very little difficulty in getting it to ring the bell even without the aid of the retrieve article.

52. *A trained dog jumping through the fire hoop.*

the hoop with cloth each time it is used, a piece of asbestos rope can be used. This will be just as effective and of course it will last almost indefinitely. A piece of cloth will, however, be the most convenient in the early stages of the training.

Do not on any account put the dog through the fire hoop if there is too much flame or if there is the slightest possibility of the dog getting injured.

The hoop should be secure to the ground so that it will not fall over when the dog is

Carrying the Fire Bucket

There should be no problem in getting your dog to carry a fire bucket containing water, providing of course that the dog is physically capable. The bucket should be made of plastic or other lightweight material, and its size will depend on the breed and size of the dog. Only a limited amount of water should be put in the bucket and the handle fastened so that it is permanently upright.

For the purpose of a demonstration, the fire hoop should be lit and immediately this is done, a dog should be sent into the arena to ring the fire bell.

Whilst the fire bell is being rung, another dog should be sent through the burning hoop. Finally another dog should run to the fire bucket which has already been placed in a convenient spot, pick it up and carry it to its handler who will throw the water over the hoop in order to extinguish the flames.

Selecting Numbered Boards

In this display exercise, wooden boards each bearing a different number are placed out in the arena. The boards, made of hardboard, can be about eight inches square (200 mm²) and each nailed to a

wooden peg about one foot (300 mm) long and one inch square (25 mm²). The numbers on the boards should be painted white so that they can easily be seen.

The commentator asks a certain dog to do some arithmetic. For example, he asks a dog to subtract seven from ten; it is then sent into the arena, picks out the No. 3 board and returns it to its handler (*photo 54*).

Instead of boards bearing numbers, names of capital cities can be painted on them, in which case the comentator asks a dog to pick out the capital of France, for example.

Orindary cloth flags of various nations can be similarly used, the dog being asked to pick out the national flag of a particular nation.

These exercises are done by scent discrimination, with the dog simply searching for its handler's scent. In other words, the particular flag that the dog is required to pick out and retrieve has been placed in the arena by the dog's handler, whilst the

53. *Ringing the fire bell.*

54. *The dog asked to take seven from ten.*

remainder have been placed out by one or more persons.

In order to teach the dog to select the flag bearing the handler's scent, it will be necessary for you to handle one of the flags for a few minutes and to ask someone else to handle a second one. Your assistant and yourself will then place out the two flags, spacing them about two feet (600 mm) apart.

Give the command 'FETCH' and more than likely the dog will fetch the one which you have handled and therefore bears your scent (*photo 55*). If it goes to the wrong flag, give the command 'NO', and as soon as the dog shows interest in the correct one, give it plenty of praise and encourage it to retrieve. Some dogs will do this exercise quite naturally and will need very little training.

Continue to use the two flags until the dog is scent-sure and is having no difficulty in selecting the correct one. When this stage has been reached, the number of flags can be gradually increased, but make sure that you only handle the one which you require your dog to fetch, and of course do not allow anyone else to touch it.

For demonstration purposes, it is a good idea to put out the flags before the demonstration begins. Place them in a row, in the ground and about two feet (600 mm) apart and of course in a position where they will not interfere with the rest of the demonstration. Do not worry about the scent going off, for it will remain on the flag for some considerable time and certainly much longer than it will take to give a demonstration.

There are many variations which can be used in this act. One which I have used at football matches at half-time is to get the dogs to indicate the half-time score.

For this purpose all that is needed is a

number of hardboard flags, as previously described, except that they will have white cardboard pinned to them with staples or drawing pins. Each flag will bear a different number which will be marked clearly with a black felt pen.

The handlers of the two dogs which are to carry out the exercise will each handle a flag but these will have a blank cardboard sheet attached. As soon as the handlers know the half-time score they will quickly mark the appropriate numbers on them and the flags will be put into the arena along with the remainder. The first dog will fetch the home side's score and the second dog the visitor's score.

The two handlers will each put out their own flags, and the rest will be put out by one or more persons. It will of course be necessary to have a commentator.

The Cycle Act

In this exercise the dog is taught to jump on to its owner's back whilst he is on a pedal cycle and to remain there whilst he cycles round the arena. It is not as difficult as it may seem, although the dog must be one which is very agile, and during the training much patience and perseverance will be needed. Not all dogs will be physically capable of performing this exercise and it must be left to the common sense of the owner.

Commence the training by placing the dog on a stout table or something similar. With your back towards the dog, bend slightly and giving the command 'UP', gently ease the dog onto your back so that its forelegs rest on your shoulders (*photo 56*). Walk about with the dog on your back, reassuring and praising it as you do

55. *The dog is asked to pick out the Scottish flag.*

56. *The dog is helped onto the back from a table.*

ground at first so that the dog does not have far to jump but as the training improves, the legs can be gradually straightened so that eventually only the back is slightly bent. Continue to walk about with the dog resting on your shoulders, reassuring and praising it as you do so. After a while the dog will begin to treat the exercise as a big game and will be eager to spring onto your shoulders on the command 'UP'.

Do not rush the training or be in too big a hurry to introduce the cycle into the exercise. The main thing is to get the dog to jump onto your back from ground level, freely and happily, and to remain there whilst you walk about. When this stage has been reached you will be able to introduce the cycle but not before.

The cycle should have the seat lowered as far as possible and preferably be one without a crossbar. Place the dog in the sit position about five paces away from you whilst you sit on the cycle with both feet resting firmly on the ground. You will need to have your back towards the dog of course.

Bend forward as far as possible, give the command 'UP' and get the dog to leap onto your back as before (*photo 57*). Do not ride the cycle at this stage but simply sit on it for a few minutes and allow the dog to remain on your back (*photo 58*). It may be necessary for you to place the left arm behind your back to support the dog's hind-quarters at first, but as it gains in confidence this will no longer be necessary. Allow the dog to jump down after a minute or so, making sure that it does not injure itself in any way.

Give the dog a rest or change to another exercise after you have been successful in getting it to jump onto your back two or possibly three times. Repeat the exercise later on but do not overdo it, otherwise the dog will lose interest.

so. After walking about for a short time, bend down and allow the dog to jump off. As usual make a fuss of it.

Continue the training until the dog is confident and quite happy to cling to your back whilst you are walking about and is showing signs of trying to get on on its own accord.

With continued training, the stage will be eventually reached when the dog will jump onto your back from the table without your assistance. You will then be able to discard the table and attempt to get the dog onto your back from ground level. It will be necessary for you to bend low to the

57. *The dog leaps on the handler's back whilst he is sitting on the cycle.*

58. *The dog rests on the handler's back, with the cycle stationary.*

59. *The dog clings to the handler's back whilst he is riding the cycle.*

As the dog gains in confidence, it will have very little difficulty in jumping onto your back whilst you are sitting on the cycle and will in fact begin to enjoy the exercise. When this stage has been reached you can now move forward on the cycle, but do not travel too far or too fast at first and keep in a fairly straight line. You should gradually increase the distance and introduce gradual turns so that eventually the dog will remain on your back whether you cycle in a straight line or tight circle (*photo 59*).

The Dog in the Pram

A very popular act, which has been carried out during dog demonstrations at public shows and other events for many years, has been the one in which a dog is pushed along in a baby's pram usually by a male handler disguised as a female. An assistant runs from behind, snatches a handbag which is hanging on the pram handle and runs away. On the command from the handler, the dog leaps from the pram, gives chase and attacks and holds the assistant or acting criminal by the right arm as in the ordinary chase and attack exercise. Very little training is required for this execise providing that the handler has good control over the dog and it has been trained to do the chase and attack exercise.

It often happens that after the dog has done this particular exercise for a few times, it begins to anticipate, and the handler has difficulty in keeping it in the pram long enough to carry out the exercise properly.

Because of this I had the idea of changing the act and substituting an ice-cream cart for the pram so that the dog is completely enclosed and cannot see what is taking place. It is also unable to jump out of the vehicle until released. The ice-cream cart, which is a hand-propelled one, can quite easily be constructed from an old pram. It should have a hinged door at the front with a quick release catch which can be operated by the handler by means of a lever situated near to the push bar (*photo 60*).

60. *Ice-cream cart constructed from an old pram. Note the door at the front and the release catch.*

The idea of the exercise is very similar to the one with the pram except that in this case the handler represents an ice-cream man and is dressed accordingly. An assistant, acting as a criminal, approaches the handler but instead of purchasing an

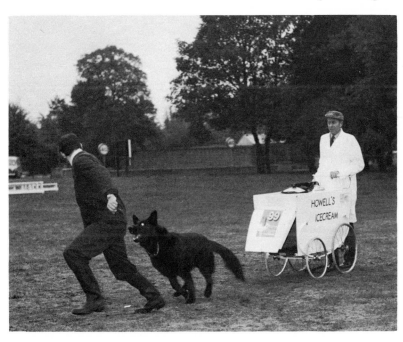

61. *Dog leaving the ice-cream cart to give chase.*

85

62. *The dog being sent to uncover 'The End' board.*

ice-cream snatches the cash bag and runs away. The handler then operates the lever and, as a result, the dog is released, gives chase and attacks the criminal (*photo 61*). The handler is then able to arrest the criminal and escort him away with the dog. A suitable commentary will be needed whilst the exercise is taking place.

'The End' Board

Having arranged and given demonstrations with dogs for the past twenty-two years, I have had the problem of trying to think up new ideas from time to time.

One simple idea which I had some years ago turned out to be extremely popular and when it is done in a neat and tidy manner, as all exercises should be, it gives a most effective finish to any dog display. I simply call it 'The End' board exercise.

The idea is to have two boards, each about three feet square (0.29 m²) and hinged together at the top so that they will stand firmly on the ground when pulled out at the base in the same manner as a blackboard easel. The boards should be painted white with black lettering on either side which should read, 'THE END: THANK YOU FOR WATCHING'. The letters should be about four inches (100 mm) in length and at least one inch (25 mm) thick, so that the words can be easily read from a distance.

Before the full demonstration begins, the board, draped in a heavy cloth or blanket, should be carried out into the arena and placed in a position where it can easily be seen by the spectators. At this stage, the spectators will be unaware of the message on the board, or in fact what the

63. *The dog uncovers 'The End' board.*

board represents. It is important, therefore, that the cloth which is covering the board is a very heavy one such as an army blanket, otherwise it could be blown off and the whole effect ruined.

At the end of the full demonstration a dog is sent forward across the arena to uncover the board and thus reveal the message (*photo 62*).

It is a very simple matter to teach a dog to uncover the board, particularly if the dog is good at retrieving.

First of all, cover the board with a blanket or other heavy drape and tie a retrieve article such as a piece of wood to the bottom of it so that the retrieve article is lying on the ground just in front of the board.

Allow the dog to see the retrieve article, and after the command 'FETCH' send the dog to retrieve it. As the dog retrieves the article, it will of course uncover the board at the same time.

The dog will quickly become accustomed to the weight of the blanket or other drape which it is pulling along, and with continued practice it should be possible to get it to retrieve the drape without the retrieve article being attached to it.

Practice the exercise in different areas and send the dog from various angles to uncover the board (*photo 63*).

87

Feeding, Grooming and General Care of the Dog

A WELL-TRAINED dog is a happy dog but if it is well looked after, it is happier still. Correct feeding, grooming and general care of your dog is of paramount importance, and any dog owner can feel justly proud of a well-trained animal which is also in first-class condition.

First of all, make sure that the dog is inoculated against the various serious infections including distemper, hardpad, hepatitis, lepto-spiral jaundice and nephritis, etc and consult your veterinary surgeon in this respect.

FEEDING

One meal per day is sufficient for an adult dog, and owners should avoid giving it tit-bits during the day. It is advisable to feed the dog at the same time each day if possible, but care should be taken not to feed it prior to any strenuous training or work. For example, a dog will not be over-enthusiastic in following a track scent if it has just had its meal, neither will it show a great deal of keenness in some of the other training exercises outlined in this book.

The dog should be fed, if possible, during the early part of the evening so that it will have plenty of time to relieve itself before being put away for the night. This will help to keep its house and kennel clean.

Some dogs put on weight very easily even though they are not overfed. If this is the case, it may help if you feed it in the mornings instead of early evening so that the daytime exercise will help to reduce its weight.

TYPE OF FOOD

Like humans, dogs need a correct and balanced diet in order to give them the necessary energy and to keep them happy and healthy.

At least half the daily diet of an adult dog should consist of protein such as meat or fish, whilst the remainder should include carbohydrates such as hound-meal and biscuits to aid the digestion, and vegetables to provide the necessary minerals and vitamins.

Although there is some value in the marrow from a marrow-bone, generally speaking, bones are not an important part of a dog's diet, although they are useful in keeping the dog happy and contented and they help to keep the teeth and gums healthy. The gnawing of a bone also assists the digestion by increasing the flow of saliva.

On no account should the dog be given any bones which splinter, such as pork or poultry, and of course they should never be fed fish unless all the bones have been carefully removed. If it is toasted, bread can be substituted for hound-meal or biscuits, as also can the various breakfast cereals.

Always make sure that the dog has an adequate supply of fresh clean drinking water, which should be changed at least once a day. Use a high-sided utensil for the water if the dog is kept in a kennel or other building and there is the slightest possibility that rats are in the vicinity. The water in a high-sided utensil will avoid the possibility of the rats urinating in the water, which is one of their traits, and passing on the very serious disease known as leptospirosis.

GROOMING

The daily grooming of the dog is of the utmost importance. It not only gives a healthy shine to the coat, but also helps to keep it free of insect pests, parasites, scurf and dust and therefore skin irritation.

The items of equipment which are necessary are a good grooming brush, a steel comb or rake, a grooming glove and a chamois leather.

Before using the brush or comb, you should give the dog a vigorous massage with both hands. This will help the circulation of the blood and at the same time loosen the dead hairs. When this has been done, you should give the coat a good brushing and then use the comb to bring out the remaining loose hairs. A further brushing, going with the grain of the hair, and a final polish with the hand glove will complete the process. The chamois leather should be used to dry the dog down, particularly under its body when it has for any reason become wet.

Great care should be taken not to over-groom the dog and spoil its appearance. It is equally important not to over-groom the dog during the cold weather, particularly if it is one of the breeds which is provided with a thick undercoat to give it the necessary protection from the cold.

BATHS

Providing that the dog is brushed and combed regularly, there should be no need to bath the dog. Bathing should be avoided if possible as it tends to soften the coat and takes out all the natural oils. It is of course sometimes essential to bath the dog when, for some reason or other, its coat has become so unclean that grooming alone will not rectify the matter.

Various shampoos are readily available but a good quality hand-soap can be used. Make sure that the coat is well rinsed afterwards, of course.

Dogs do not particularly like the bath water to be too warm and for that reason, a warm bath for a dog would be 80°F (26.7°C) whilst a hot one would be about 100°F (37.8°C).

THE EYES

When grooming the dog, you should examine the eyes for any pus or matter which may have formed. This may simply be caused by the dog being in a draught or, alternatively, it could be an eye ailment, an injury to the eye or the signs of some other illness. If only one eye is affected, however, it is fairly certain that there is nothing seriously wrong and that it is simply a local cause. If the pus is not removed, the eye could quite easily become ulcerated. A clean pad of cotton-wool dipped in clean warm water can be used to

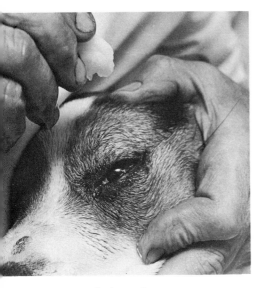

Cleaning up a discharge from an eye.

THE TEETH

Make sure that the dog's teeth are clean and free from tartar, also that the gums are firm and healthy. If the teeth are loose or in very bad condition, they should be removed by a veterinary surgeon. Bad teeth can be caused by in-correct feeding in some cases or following some disease such as distemper. Normally, the dog's teeth can be kept clean by ordinary brushing with a soft tooth brush and the use of powder or paste. The dog should be given a large beef bone to gnaw at from time to time and this will help to prevent any tartar and it will assist also in keeping the gums firm and healthy.

THE EARS

Examine the ear cavity for any sign of irritation, foreign bodies or growths. A dog with ear trouble will usually shake its head and quite frequently hold it on one

clean out the eyes, but it should be done with great care so as not to injure the eyes or cause any further irritation. If, in addition to the discharge from the eyes, the dog appears to be ill or out of condition, you should consult your veterinary surgeon.

THE NAILS

Examine the dog's nails. If they are too long they can cause discomfort, particularly when the dog is on a hard surface such as a roadway. If the nails need cutting, use a strong pair of nail cutters specially made for the purpose but be extremely careful not to cut them too low and therefore damge the quick. With nails which are white, the quick can easily be seen and as a result it is a fairly simple matter to cut them without going too low. If, however, the nails are black, the quick cannot easily be seen and it is strongly advisable to have the nails cut by your veterinary surgeon.

Only the experienced dog breeder or veterinary surgeon should clip nails.

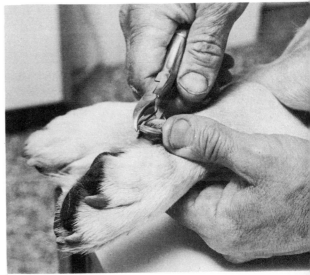

side. Do not poke about inside the ear if you suspect any infection but consult your veterinary surgeon.

THE FEET

Make sure that there are no foreign bodies in the pads and that the pads and feet are free from injury and soreness. Sore pads are often caused by too much exercise on hard road surfaces or by the dog walking over some form of irritant.

It sometimes happens that a dog will slice off a pad completely on broken glass or the like and if this happens many owners fear the worst. If it should happen to your dog, do not worry too much, for it will quickly grow a new pad, providing that the pad is kept clean and free from infection.

LAMENESS

When a dog is lame but there is no definite sign of injury, the inexperienced owner may have some difficulty in determining which foot or leg is injured. One way to find out is to watch the movement of the dog as it will drop or nod its head on the uninjured side.

THE NOSE

The nose should be moist and cool, but it does not necessarily follow that a warm or dry nose always denotes that the dog is sick. Watch out for any discharge from the nose, as this may indicate that the dog is unwell.

TAKING THE TEMPERATURE

The normal temperature of a dog is 101.5°F (38.6°C) when the temperature is taken by means of the thermometer being inserted in the rectum. If it is taken by placing the thermometer in the folds of the skin inside the thigh, the reading should be one degree lower, although this method is not entirely reliable. Do not attempt to take the dog's temperature in the mouth, as serious injury could be caused by the dog biting and breaking the thermometer.

The thermometer, which is called a clinical one, is the same as the one used for humans and it is advisable for all dog owners to have one.

Before the thermometer is used, it should be greased with vaseline and given a good shake. It should then be placed in the rectum so that it penetrates for about one and a half inches (38 mm) and left in the rectum for half a minute. The dog should be kept as quiet as possible whilst the temperature is being taken as it would be an easy matter for the dog to break the thermometer and injure itself. With care and sensible use, there should be no problems, however.

If, for some reason or other it is not possible to take the temperature by the rectum, it will be necessary to take it by placing the thermometer in the folds of the skin inside the thigh as mentioned earlier. In this case, the thermometer should be left there for a minute and a half and not for half a minute as before. Remember also that the normal temperature will be 100.5°F (38.1°C) when taken in this manner and not 101.5°F (38.6°). Always make sure that the thermometer is cleaned and sterilised after use.

TAKING THE PULSE

The pulse rate can be taken on the inside of the thigh on the femoral artery. The beats per minute vary according to the size of the dog and they can vary from 70 to 100 times per minute. For example, with an Alsatian the beats would be about

80, whilst with some of the toy breeds it would be about 100. When a dog is ill it is normal for the beats to increase but in some cases such as pneumonia or diseases affecting the heart, the beats can drop dramatically.

ADMINISTERING TABLETS AND MEDICINE

It is often necessary for the dog owner to administer tablets and liquid medicine to his or her dog and in many cases owners have a complete lack of knowledge as to how this should be done.

To administer tablets you should stand with the dog on your left side, place the left hand on the dog's muzzle and with the dog's head slightly raised, press fairly firmly on the cheek and between the teeth to cause the dog to open its mouth. If you are firm and you are able to keep up the pressure, there will be no problem in getting the dog to open its mouth and it

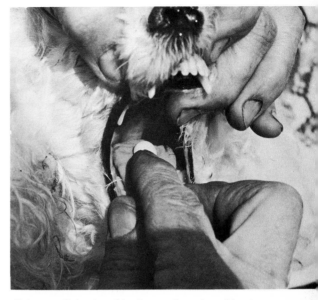

Giving medicine in tablet form; place the tablet over the back of the tongue.

will not be able to bite you. If you are hesitant and unsure of yourself, the dog will be wary and you will probably have difficulty when you try again.

Now with your right hand and the tablet between the thumb and forefinger, place the tablet into the dog's mouth and as far back as possible into the back of the throat. Close the dog's mouth quickly and stroke the dog under the chin in a downwards movement, putting on some slight pressure as you do so to cause the dog to swallow the tablet. It is possible to administer two or more tablets together, providing of course that you are able to hold them between the thumb and forefinger. It is emphasised that the tablets should be pushed well back into the throat and not simply dropped into the dog's mouth.

Liquid can be administered to a dog by means of a bottle or a spoon. It is much easier to administer it from a bottle, however, and there is less likelihood of the

Using a spoon to adminster a liquid medicine.

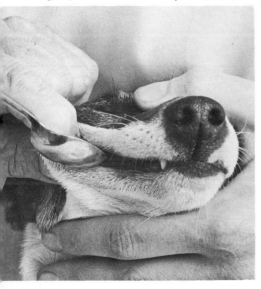

93

liquid being spilled. To give the dog liquid from a glass bottle, you should again stand with the dog on your left side. Place the left hand around the whole of the muzzle this time and with the dog's head slightly raised, with your right hand place the neck of the bottle inside the cheek, pouring a small amount into the cheek cavity or pouch. There should be no problem in getting the dog to swallow the liquid.

A much easier method, however, is to use a plastic bottle instead of a glass one. Because there is no possibility of the dog biting the bottle and breaking it, the neck of the bottle can be placed directly into the mouth. In the same manner as described for the administering of tablets, stand with the dog on your left side. With the left hand placed over the muzzle and the dog's head slightly raised, press firmly on the cheek and between the teeth to cause the dog to open its mouth slightly. With the right hand, press the neck of the bottle into the mouth on one side and allow the liquid to slowly run into the mouth and down the throat. Do not overdo this as it may cause the dog to choke.

Liquid can be given to a dog in the same manner by using a spoon but as previously mentioned, there is more likelihood of the liquid being spilled if a spoon is used and by far the best method is by use of a plastic bottle.

CARING FOR A SICK DOG

When your dog is ill it should be kept in a well ventilated room at a constant room temperature of 60°F (15.6°C). It should not be allowed to move about inside or outside the room and you should not constantly fuss and pester the dog but allow it to be as quiet and restful as possible. Although the room should be well ventilated, it should be free of any draughts.

It is a good idea to use newspaper as bedding for a sick dog which is kept in the house, as plenty of this will help to keep the dog warm and of course the paper can be burned when fouled and easily replaced with a clean supply.

On no account should a sick dog be kept with other dogs whether or not they are sick or healthy.

If a dog is one that is kept outside in a kennel or other building, it should be kept warm in the same manner as a dog kept in the house. There will probably be no heating system but it may be possible to fix up a portable fire of some kind, and if this is so, it will be a great help. If, however, a fire is not possible, you should make sure that there are no draughts and that the dog has a good warm bed to lie on. A thick bed of clean straw is probably the best as this too can easily be burned and replaced with a clean supply. The kennel or building will need to be kept at a temperature of about 55°F (12.8°C).

One of the most important aspects of nursing a sick dog is cleanliness. The room, feeding utensils, the dog and yourself must be kept scrupulously clean at all times, and any items such as cotton-wool used to clean the dog's eyes and mouth should be burned after use and on no account used a second time.

Take the dog's temperature at least twice a day at the same time each day and keep a strict record of this. Keep a similar record of the pulse rate.

A sick dog will probably be reluctant to accept food, and if this is so, it will be necessary to spoon feed it when feeding semi-solid food and to use the plastic bottle as described earlier for administering any liquid food.

Milk with the white of an egg, beef tea, fish soup and similar nourishing liquids of this kind are extremely good and they will help to keep up the dog's strength, but it will not be possible to give them to the dog in any large quantities. The dog should be fed in this way every few hours during the day and night.

It will be much better if the dog will take the food itself of course, and when it will do this, other tempting foods can be given. There are a number of prepared invalid foods which are available these days and they are extremely good.

After feeding the dog you should always clean its mouth with a pad of cotton-wool, remembering to burn the pad afterwards.

WHEN A DOG IS INJURED

It often happens that a dog which is injured will cause further injury to itself by biting at the injured part, tearing out stitches and pulling off any wound or other dressings. If this happens, it can be a great worry to the owner as either the healing is delayed or further infection can result. The owner is able to check the dog when he or she is present of course, but it is a different matter when the dog is left entirely on its own particularly at night-time.

There are specially-made high collars which can be placed on the dog's neck to prevent it from turning or bending its head, but naturally the ordinary dog owner does not usually have equipment of this kind readily available. Improvision is therefore necessary and one often finds that the simple methods are often the best.

You will need an ordinary plastic bucket such as those available in all sizes from supermarkets and general stores. First of all, you must select one which appears to be the most suitable size to fit over the dog's head.

Cut out the bottom of the bucket and after you have trimmed the bucket to the correct size to form a high collar, take off

To stop a dog biting itself, place a plastic bucket (with bottom cut away) over its head.

the handle. When you are satisfied that the dog is unable to move its head sufficiently to damage the wound, you should carefully tape the newly cut edges with some kind of adhesive tape so that they will not injure or irritate the dog's neck in any way.

The bucket should be fastened to the dog's collar, which should be an ordinary flat one and not a check collar or chain.

You will of course have to be guided by the size of your dog when selecting the type of bucket to be used, but because of the very many sizes available it will be more than likely that you will be able to get one to suit your particular needs. It may be necessary to use a child's toy bucket for the smaller breed of dog.

Do not leave the collar on the dog for long periods unless it is absolutely necessary, and make sure that the collar is a good and comfortable fit and that it will not be possible for the dog to shake it off.

95

MUZZLING A DOG

It is always a good idea to purchase a muzzle which is the correct size and type for your dog but, again, not all dog owners do this and of course not all dogs need to be muzzled.

There are occasions, however, when even a good-tempered dog has to be muzzled, particularly if it has been injured or needs some kind of attention which it dislikes. Some dogs, for example, do not like to have their nails cut, especially if this is done by a stranger.

If a muzzle is not available, a length of strong tape or bandage will suffice. Hold each end of the tape (one end in each hand) across the top of the dog's nose and then tie it tightly under the dog's chin. Take the two ends round the head at the back of the ears and again tie the two ends firmly together. Make sure that the dog's mouth is firmly closed but be equally careful to check that the dog is able to breath properly, particularly if is one of the breeds with a short pug nose.

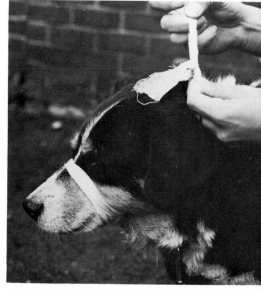

6. *A tape muzzle for restraining a dog.*

With practice, it will be possible to muzzle your dog in this way in just a few seconds, in fact even before the dog has time to realise what is happening.

The photographs reproduced in the Appendix are taken from
THE TV VET DOG BOOK, by the TV Vet, published by Farming Press Ltd.

Index

Take good care of your dog

THE TV VET

DOG BOOK

tells you how

Hardback, 9½" x 7", 208 pages

The "TV Vet", one of Britain's leading veterinary surgeons, uses more than 380 striking photographs and easy-to-follow text to deal with dog ailments and conditions, and also gives many helpful hints. A vital reference book for all dog owners and breeders.

FARMING PRESS LIMITED
Wharfedale Road, Ipswich
IP1 4LG, Suffolk